The ABC's of COOKING

Page 2

Contents

D0586256

Tools
Page 4

The ABC's of COOKING

Welcome to The Pampered Chef's cookbook for kids. If you're like most kids, you like to eat, especially foods you make yourself. Adults have been using Pampered Chef kitchen tools and equipment for years, but now it's your turn. Whether baking cookies, sharing snacks with friends or helping make dinner, you'll discover cooking is delicious, easy and fun with kid-friendly tools from The Pampered Chef.

Getting Started

Before you begin, there are a few simple steps to follow:

- First choose a recipe you'd like to try. Check to see if you have all of the ingredients, in the amounts you need, on hand. Write down anything you don't have. Grocery shopping from a list is the easiest way.

- Get permission from an adult to make sure it's a good time for cooking.

- Wash your hands with soap and warm water. Germs can easily be passed to other people through food you prepare.

- Use an apron to keep your clothes clean, and pull back long hair.

- Gather all the ingredients and tools listed and any other needed supplies. If you don't have a specific Pampered Chef tool, just ask an adult to help find a substitute.

- Use The Pampered Chef **Clock/Timer** to follow cooking and baking times exactly.

Reading the Recipe

When you cook, reading and following a recipe is important in order to get tasty results.

- Before cooking, read through your recipe carefully. These recipes have been written especially for you, but ask an adult about anything you don't understand.

- You'll find the recipe ingredients listed in blue type and Pampered Chef tools listed in red type. If you aren't familiar with a tool, refer to the section, Cool Tools, on pages 4-5.

- Some recipe steps start with the words "Adult help." If a recipe calls for adult help, be sure an adult is available while you are cooking.

Playing it Safe

To have fun in the kitchen follow some easy safety rules:

- Find a clear, clean space on the kitchen counter or table where you can work.

- Ask an adult to help you learn how to use the many kid-friendly cutting, slicing and chopping tools from The Pampered Chef: **My Safe Cutter™, Kitchen Shears, Egg Slicer Plus®, Garnisher** or **Crinkle Cutter, Apple Wedger, Food Chopper** and **Apple Peeler/Corer/Slicer.**

- Do slicing and chopping on a **Cutting Board.** Place The Pampered Chef **Grip-Net Pad** under your cutting board to keep the board from slipping while you cut.

- If handling raw meat or poultry, wash your hands, cutting board and tools in hot, soapy water immediately after you're done to prevent spreading harmful bacteria.

- When cooking on top of the stove, turn handles of

saucepans and skillets toward the middle or back of the stove, so you won't bump the handles and spill hot food.

- **Oven Mitts** should be used for taking foods out of the oven or microwave. Have a **Nonstick Cooling Rack, Oven Pad** or **Stoneware Trivet** ready for hot cookware or stoneware.

- Try to keep the kitchen neat while you're cooking. Wipe up any spills on the floor right away so you won't slip and fall.

- Let hot stoneware cool completely before washing to avoid breaking.

Measuring Know How

Good cooks are careful to measure their ingredients accurately.

- *Liquids:* Measure liquids such as water and milk in The Pampered Chef **Measure-All® Cup**. The cup should be placed on a level surface and you should bend down so that your eyes are even with the measurement mark you are using. The liquid should be level with this mark.

- *Dry Ingredients:* Use the **Adjustable Scoop** for measuring dry ingredients, such as flour and sugar. By adjusting the scoop, you can measure any amounts you need with

just one tool. Lightly spoon the ingredient into the scoop, just a little above the top, then level it off with the straight edge of a knife.

- *Brown Sugar:* Adjust the scoop for the amount you need, then firmly press brown sugar into the scoop with your fingers until level with the top. When you dump out the brown sugar, it will hold its shape.

- *Peanut Butter:* Adjust the **Measure-All® Cup** for the amount you need, then pack with peanut butter. Level the top, then use the plunger to push out peanut butter.

- *Butter and Margarine:* These come in sticks with helpful markings on the wrappers for tablespoons, ¼ cup and ⅓ cup. One stick equals ½ cup. Use **My Safe Cutter™** to cut the wrapped stick for the amount you need. For best results in baking, use butter or margarine.

- *Seasonings:* Adjust an **Adjustable Measuring Spoon** for the amount you need, then dip the spoon into the ingredient to fill. Level off.

Cook Up Some Fun

Cooking is fun, but all cooks make mistakes, sometimes. Don't

worry. Even the "mistakes" can taste pretty good. So, what are you waiting for? The Pampered Chef *Kids in the Kitchen* cookbook has all kinds of snacks to share with friends like chocolate caramel dip or fruit-flavored ices. You'll find sleeping late isn't as much fun as making French toast sticks. Would you like to make a pineapple upside-down cake or banana cream pie? How about a giant cookie that looks like a pizza? It's time to head for the kitchen to cook up some fun!

Kitchen Math

If you have questions about measuring ingredients, this chart can help.

Dash = a few sprinkles

3 teaspoons = 1 tablespoon

4 tablespoons = ¼ cup

5 tablespoons + 1 teaspoon = ⅓ cup

8 tablespoons = ½ cup

16 tablespoons = 1 cup

1 cup = ½ pint = 8 liquid ounces

2 cups = 1 pint = 16 liquid ounces

2 pints = 4 cups = 32 liquid ounces = 1 quart

4 quarts = 128 liquid ounces = 1 gallon

Cool Tools

Measure-All® Cup

Egg Slicer Plus®

My Safe Cutter

Vegetable Peeler

The Corer™

Food Chopper

V-Shaped Cutter

Nylon Masher

Lemon Zester/Scorer

Pizza Cutter

Ice Shaver with Tubs

Nylon Tool Set

Deluxe Cheese Grater

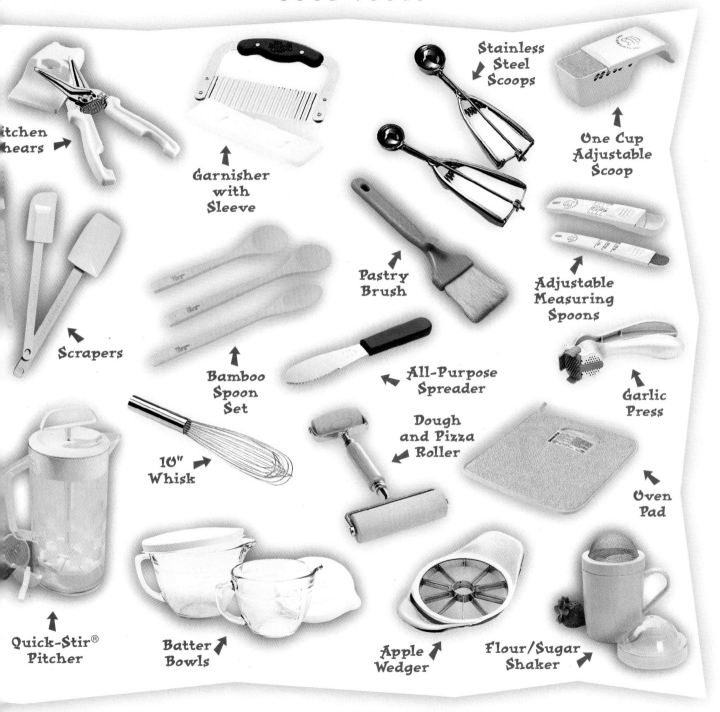

Kitchen Shears

Garnisher with Sleeve

Stainless Steel Scoops

One Cup Adjustable Scoop

Scrapers

Bamboo Spoon Set

Pastry Brush

Adjustable Measuring Spoons

All-Purpose Spreader

Garlic Press

10" Whisk

Dough and Pizza Roller

Oven Pad

Quick-Stir® Pitcher

Batter Bowls

Apple Wedger

Flour/Sugar Shaker

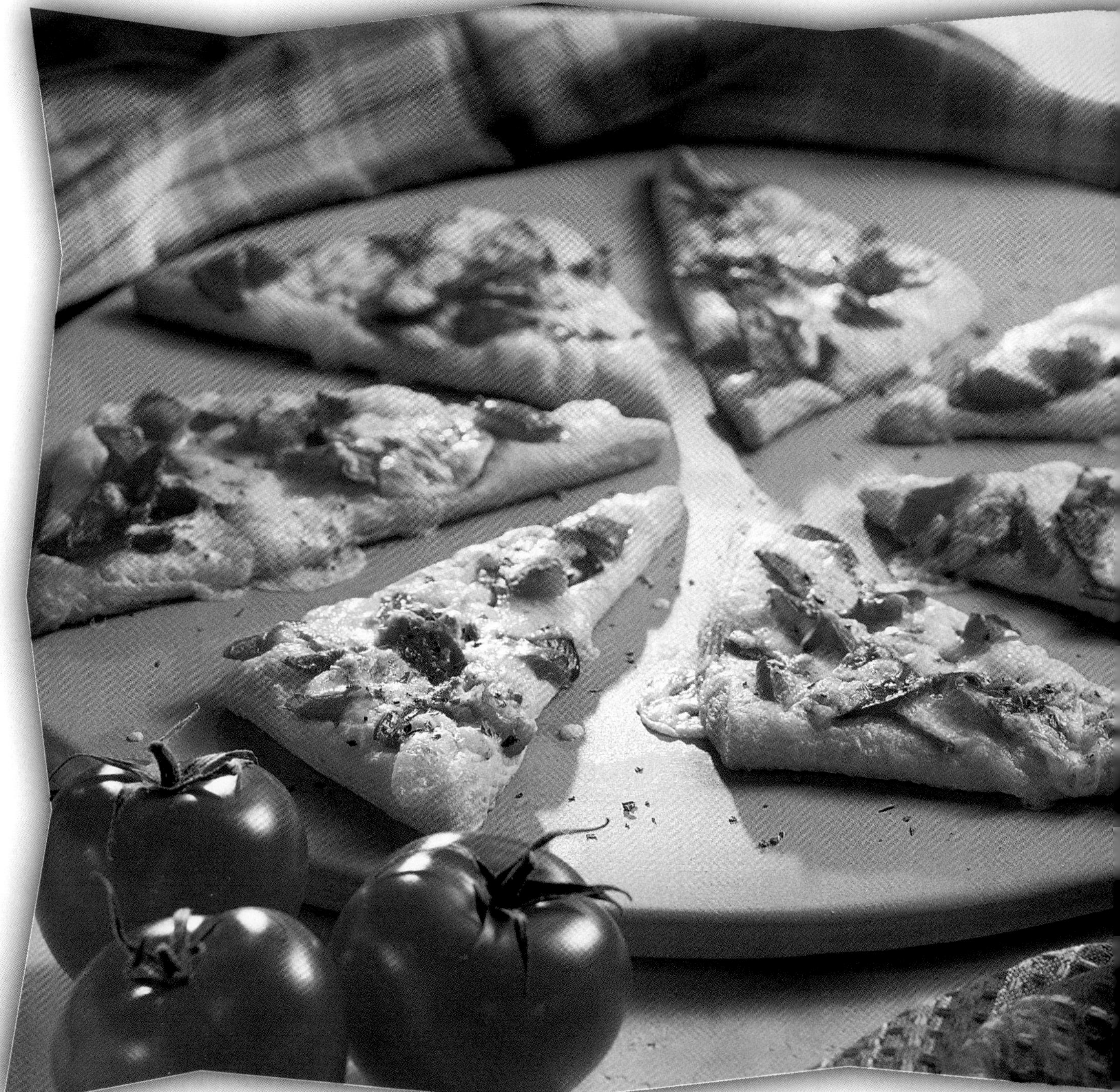

Pizza By The Slice p. 8

Lip-Smack'n Snacks

Munch, crunch, dip and sip...
Grab some friends
and have some fun.

Pizza By The Slice

INVITE A FRIEND OVER FOR A SLICE OF PIPING HOT PIZZA
AND LET THE FUN BEGIN!

MAKES 8 SERVINGS

Ingredients:

- I MEDIUM TOMATO
- 2 OUNCES SLICED HARD SALAMI (ABOUT 6 SLICES)
- 2 OUNCES MOZZARELLA CHEESE, SHREDDED (½ CUP)
- I PACKAGE (8 OUNCES) REFRIGERATED CRESCENT ROLLS
- ½ TEASPOON DRIED OREGANO LEAVES

Tools:

ADJUSTABLE SCOOP

ADJUSTABLE MEASURING SPOON

QUIKUT PARING KNIFE

TOMATO CORER

18" X 12" GROOVED CUTTING BOARD

FOOD CHOPPER

PIZZA CUTTER

DELUXE CHEESE GRATER

FLAT BAKING STONE WITH OVEN-TO-TABLE RACK

OVEN MITTS

MINI-SERVING SPATULA

1 Preheat oven to 375°F. Remove stem end of tomato with **Tomato Corer**. On **Cutting Board**, cut tomato into several large chunks using **Quikut Paring Knife** then coarsely chop using **Food Chopper**.

2 Stack salami slices, two at a time, and cut into small wedges using **Pizza Cutter**.

3 Shred cheese using **Deluxe Cheese Grater** fitted with coarse shredding drum.

4 Unroll crescent dough on cutting board and separate into 8 triangles using Pizza Cutter. Arrange the triangles on a flat **Baking Stone** so they do not touch.

5 Sprinkle triangles with equal amounts of tomato, salami, cheese and oregano. Place Baking Stone in **Oven-To-Table Rack**.

6 *Adult help:* Bake 15-18 minutes or until edges are golden brown. Using **Oven Mitts**, remove from oven. Serve warm using **Mini-Serving Spatula**.

Approximately 260 calories and 16 grams of fat per serving

Berry Banana Fruit Smoothies

YOU'LL GO BANANAS OVER THIS COOL
AND REFRESHING FRUIT DRINK!

MAKES 2 SERVINGS (ABOUT 1 CUP EACH)

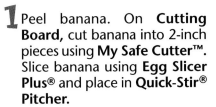

Ingredients:

1 MEDIUM RIPE BANANA
1 CONTAINER (8 OUNCES)
   RASPBERRY OR STRAWBERRY
   YOGURT
1 CAN (6 OUNCES) UNSWEETENED
   PINEAPPLE JUICE (¾ CUP)

Tools:

MY SAFE CUTTER™
13" X 9" CUTTING BOARD
EGG SLICER PLUS®
QUICK-STIR® PITCHER
NYLON MASHER

1 Peel banana. On **Cutting Board**, cut banana into 2-inch pieces using **My Safe Cutter™**. Slice banana using **Egg Slicer Plus®** and place in **Quick-Stir® Pitcher.**

2 Using **Nylon Masher**, mash banana until fairly smooth.

3 Add yogurt and juice to pitcher. Mix well with plunger. Pour into 2 drinking glasses and enjoy.

Approximately 220 calories and 2 grams of fat per serving

Orangana Smoothies:

Use vanilla yogurt instead of the raspberry yogurt and ¾ cup orange juice instead of the pineapple juice.

Cook's Tips:

WHEN A BANANA GETS BROWN "FRECKLES" ON ITS SKIN, IT'S RIPE, FLAVORFUL AND READY TO BE USED IN A SMOOTHIE.

DON'T BE AFRAID TO EXPERIMENT WITH OTHER FLAVORS OF YOGURT AND JUICE IN OUR SMOOTHIE RECIPE. SMOOTHIES AREN'T JUST FOR SNACKTIME. HAVING A SMOOTHIE FOR BREAKFAST IS A TASTY AND NUTRITIOUS WAY TO START YOUR DAY.

Tool Tip:

BE SURE TO TURN THE LID ON THE **QUICK-STIR® PITCHER** TO THE CLOSED POSITION BEFORE MIXING INGREDIENTS.

Flower Power Snacks

MAYBE IT'S THE SPECIAL SHAPE THAT MAKES THESE OPEN-FACED SANDWICHES TASTE SO GOOD!

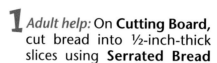

Ingredients:

FLOWER POWER FRENCH BREAD
(RECIPE FOLLOWS)

MAYONNAISE, MUSTARD OR
SOFTENED BUTTER (YOUR CHOICE)

BOLOGNA SLICES

AMERICAN CHEESE SLICES

CHERRY TOMATOES

PICKLE FANS AND CUCUMBER
CARTWHEELS (SEE COOK'S TIPS)

Tools:

SERRATED BREAD KNIFE

13" X 9" CUTTING BOARD

ALL-PURPOSE SPREADER

FLOWER BREAD TUBE

KITCHEN SPRITZER

OVEN MITTS

NONSTICK COOLING RACK

QUIKUT PARING KNIFE

LEMON ZESTER/SCORER

1 *Adult help:* On **Cutting Board**, cut bread into ½-inch-thick slices using **Serrated Bread Knife.**

2 Using **All-Purpose Spreader**, spread bread slices with mayonnaise, mustard or softened butter.

3 Cut bologna and cheese slices into flower shapes using **Flower Bread Tube** and place 1 bologna and 1 cheese cutout over each bread slice.

4 Cut cherry tomatoes in half and add to centers of flowers. Decorate with mustard, if desired.

Approximately 200 calories and 15 grams of fat per serving (1 sandwich)

Cook's Tips:

TO MAKE PICKLE FANS FOR STEMS, USE SWEET PICKLES ABOUT 3 INCHES LONG. PLACE PICKLE ON ITS SIDE. USING QUIKUT PARING KNIFE, MAKE ¼-INCH-WIDE CUTS DOWN LENGTH OF THE PICKLE, STARTING A LITTLE BELOW THE END. TAKE CARE TO KEEP EVERYTHING ATTACHED AT END SO YOU CAN FAN IT OUT.

TO MAKE CUCUMBER CARTWHEELS FOR FLOWER CENTERS, USE A SMALL CUCUMBER. USING SCORING HOLE OF **LEMON ZESTER/SCORER**, REMOVE THIN STRIPS OF PEEL LENGTHWISE TO CREATE A STRIPED EFFECT ALL THE WAY AROUND THE CUCUMBER. SLICE CUCUMBER INTO ¼-INCH-THICK ROUNDS WITH QUIKUT PARING KNIFE.

Flower Power French Bread

MAKES 24 SLICES

Ingredients:

1 PACKAGE (11 OUNCES)
REFRIGERATED FRENCH
BREAD DOUGH

1 *Adult help:* Adjust oven racks so **Flower Bread Tube** can stand upright in oven. Preheat oven to 375°F.

2 Lightly spray inside of bread tube and caps with vegetable oil using **Kitchen Spritzer**. Place cap on bottom of bread tube. Place dough in tube; cap top.

3 *Adult help:* Bake upright, 50-60 minutes. (Don't worry if cap pops off top.) Using **Oven Mitts**, carefully remove bread tube to **Nonstick Cooling Rack**. Let bread cool in tube 10 minutes. Remove bread and cool completely.

Approximately 30 calories and 0 grams of fat per serving (1 slice)

Flower Power Snacks, Fruit Jewels p. 12

Fruit Jewels

PUT SOME SPARKLE INTO SNACKTIME WITH THESE FRUITY GELATIN JEWELS!

MAKES 8 SERVINGS (24 SNACKS)

Ingredients:

2 PACKAGES (3 OUNCES EACH) GELATIN DESSERT (CHOOSE 2 OF YOUR FAVORITE FLAVORS)

1⅓ CUPS WATER

⅔-1 CUP FRUIT (YOU CHOOSE): FRESH SMALL STRAWBERRIES (CUT IN HALF), BLUEBERRIES OR SEEDLESS GRAPES, OR CANNED MANDARIN ORANGE SEGMENTS OR PINEAPPLE TIDBITS, DRAINED

Tools:

MEASURE-ALL® CUP
COVERED MICRO-COOKER®
SUPER SCRAPER
1-QT. BATTER BOWL
DELUXE MINI-MUFFIN PAN
MY SAFE CUTTER™
13" X 9" CUTTING BOARD
CITRUS PEELER

1 Empty 1 package of gelatin into **1-Qt. Batter Bowl.**

2 Pour ⅔ cup water into **Covered Micro-Cooker®.** Microwave on HIGH 1-2 minutes or until boiling.

3 *Adult help:* Pour boiling water into Batter Bowl and stir with **Super Scraper** until gelatin is completely dissolved, about 3 minutes.

4 Place 1-3 pieces of fruit (depending on size) in each of 12 cups of **Deluxe Mini-Muffin Pan.** Pour gelatin over fruit. (The fruit will float to the top of the cup.)

5 *Adult help:* Repeat steps #1-#4 with second package of gelatin, remaining ⅔ cup water and fruit to fill remaining 12 cups of Mini-Muffin Pan.

6 Refrigerate 2 hours or until firm. Run flat end of **Citrus Peeler** around cup to loosen gelatin snack.

Approximately 80 calories and 0 grams of fat per serving (3 snacks)

Cook's Tip:

YOU CAN MIX AND MATCH ANY OF THE FRUITS WITH ANY FLAVOR GELATIN, BUT WE LIKE THE JEWELED APPEARANCE OF MATCHING FRUIT AND GELATIN COLORS. FOR EXAMPLE, USE GREEN GRAPES WITH LIME FLAVOR GELATIN, STRAWBERRIES WITH STRAWBERRY FLAVOR GELATIN OR PINEAPPLE TIDBITS WITH LEMON FLAVOR GELATIN.

Tool Tip:

THE NONSTICK COATING ON OUR **DELUXE MINI-MUFFIN PAN** MAKES FOR EASY RELEASE OF THESE GELATIN SNACKS FROM THE CUPS.

Munch a Bunch Snack Mix

PACK A PUNCH IN YOUR LUNCH WITH THIS
CRUNCHY SNACK MIX COMBO.

MAKES 18 SERVINGS (9 CUPS)

Ingredients:

5 CUPS BITE-SIZE CRISPY CORN
    AND RICE CEREAL
2 CUPS CHOW MEIN NOODLES
1 CUP HONEY ROASTED PEANUTS
¼ CUP (½ STICK) BUTTER OR
    MARGARINE
1 TABLESPOON SOY SAUCE
1 TEASPOON SEASONED SALT
1 CUP GOLDEN OR DARK RAISINS

Tools:

ADJUSTABLE SCOOP
ADJUSTABLE MEASURING SPOONS
9" X 13" BAKER
MIX 'N SCRAPER®
MY SAFE CUTTER™
COVERED MICRO-COOKER®
OVEN MITTS
NONSTICK COOLING RACK

1 Preheat oven to 350°F. In **9" x 13" Baker**, combine cereal, chow mein noodles and peanuts using **Mix 'N Scraper®**.

2 Place butter in **Covered Micro-Cooker®**. Microwave on HIGH 1 minute or until melted. Stir in soy sauce and seasoned salt.

3 Pour butter mixture over cereal mixture and gently stir with scraper until cereal mixture is evenly coated.

4 *Adult help:* Bake 15 minutes. Using **Oven Mitts**, remove Baker to **Nonstick Cooling Rack.**

5 Gently stir raisins into cereal mixture. Cool completely. Store in airtight container.

Approximately 170 calories and 7 grams
of fat per serving (½ cup)

Cook's Tip:

DID YOU KNOW BOTH GOLDEN RAISINS AND DARK RAISINS ARE GRAPES THAT HAVE BEEN DRIED, EITHER NATURALLY BY THE SUN OR BY ARTIFICIAL HEAT? IF YOU DON'T LIKE RAISINS MUCH, JUST LEAVE THEM OUT.

Brain Freeze Banana Split

Brain Freeze

YOU'LL LOVE THE SMOOTH TEXTURE AND FRUITY
FLAVORS OF THESE ICY HOMEMADE TREATS!

MAKES 9 SERVINGS

Ingredients:

¾ CUP FROZEN GRAPE JUICE
   CONCENTRATE

3 CONTAINERS (8 OUNCES EACH)
   VANILLA YOGURT

Tools:

SUPER SCRAPER

MEASURE-ALL® CUP

CLASSIC 2-QT. BATTER BOWL

10" WHISK

ICE SHAVER WITH TUBS

CHILLZANNE® MINI-BOWL

MEDIUM STAINLESS STEEL SCOOP

MY SAFE CUTTER™

13" X 9" CUTTING BOARD

1 In **Classic 2-Qt. Batter Bowl,** mix frozen concentrate with **10" Whisk** until smooth and slightly thawed. Whisk in yogurt until completely blended.

2 Divide mixture evenly among 3 **Ice Shaver Tubs** and cover with lids. Place tubs and **Chillzanne® Mini-Bowl** in freezer and freeze until firm (about 6 hours).

3 Place Chillzanne® Mini-Bowl under **Ice Shaver** to catch shavings. Remove frozen mixture from tubs and shave with Ice Shaver. Scoop shaved ice into serving dishes using medium **Stainless Steel Scoop.**

Approximately 120 calories and 2 grams of fat per serving

Pink Punch Brain Freeze:
Use frozen fruit punch concentrate instead of grape juice concentrate.

Pineapple Brain Freeze:
Use frozen pineapple or pineapple-banana juice concentrate instead of grape juice concentrate.

Brain Freeze Banana Splits:
Make 1 tub each of Brain Freeze, Pink Punch Brain Freeze and Pineapple Brain Freeze using 1 container vanilla yogurt and ¼ cup juice concentrate for each tub. Using **My Safe Cutter™,** cut 4 peeled bananas in half lengthwise. Place 2 banana halves in each of 4 banana split dishes. Shave mixtures with Ice Shaver. Top each banana with 1 scoop each of all 3 flavors. Decorate with strawberries, maraschino cherries or nuts, if you like. Makes 4 servings.

Cook's Tip:

FROZEN JUICE CONCENTRATES USUALLY COME IN 12-OUNCE CANS. WHEN USING ¾ CUP CONCENTRATE FOR THIS RECIPE, THE REMAINING JUICE CONCENTRATE CAN BE MIXED WITH 2⅔ CUPS WATER IN OUR **QUICK-STIR®** **PITCHER.**

Fluffy Peanut Butter Dip

YOU'LL FLIP OVER THIS CREAMY DIP MADE WITH PEANUT BUTTER, VANILLA YOGURT AND WHIPPED TOPPING. CRISP APPLE OR PEAR WEDGES MAKE GREAT DIPPERS.

MAKES 12 SERVINGS (1⅔ CUPS)

Ingredients:

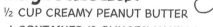

½ CUP CREAMY PEANUT BUTTER

1 CONTAINER (8 OUNCES) VANILLA YOGURT

⅛ TEASPOON GROUND CINNAMON (IF DESIRED)

½ CUP THAWED FROZEN WHIPPED TOPPING

APPLES OR PEARS FOR DIPPING

Tools:

SUPER SCRAPER

MEASURE-ALL® CUP

1-QT. BATTER BOWL

ADJUSTABLE MEASURING SPOON

10" WHISK

CHILLZANNE® MINI-BOWL

APPLE WEDGER

13" X 9" CUTTING BOARD

1 Place peanut butter, yogurt and cinnamon in **1-Qt. Batter Bowl**; stir with **10" Whisk** until thoroughly blended.

2 Using whisk, gently stir whipped topping into peanut butter mixture until blended.

3 Using **Super Scraper**, put dip in chilled **Chillzanne® Mini-Bowl** for serving and storing.

4 For dippers, cut apples or pears with **Apple Wedger** on **Cutting Board**.

Approximately 90 calories and 6 grams of fat per serving (about 2 tablespoons of dip)

Fluffy Strawberry Dip:

Leave out the peanut butter. Prepare recipe according to directions except use strawberry yogurt instead of vanilla yogurt. Makes 10 servings (1¼ cups).

Tool Tips:

IT'S EASY TO MEASURE PEANUT BUTTER WITH OUR UNIQUE **MEASURE-ALL® CUP**. THE PLUNGER DESIGN LETS YOU SHOOT THE PEANUT BUTTER RIGHT OUT OF THE CUP AND INTO YOUR BATTER BOWL.

USING THE **APPLE WEDGER** IS A SUPER SPEEDY WAY TO CUT APPLES AND PEARS FOR SNACKING. JUST STAND APPLE OR PEAR UPRIGHT ON A CUTTING BOARD, CENTER APPLE WEDGER OVER STEM OF FRUIT AND PRESS STRAIGHT DOWN. YOU'LL GET PERFECT WEDGES WITHOUT THE CORE EVERY TIME.

Fluffy Peanut Butter Dip

Alphabet Bread Sticks

Alphabet Bread Sticks

YOU CAN ROLL 'EM, SHAPE 'EM AND BAKE 'EM — BUT EATING 'EM IS THE BEST!

MAKES 8 SERVINGS

Ingredients:

- 2 TABLESPOONS BUTTER OR MARGARINE
- 1 OUNCE FRESH PARMESAN CHEESE, GRATED (¼ CUP)
- 1 PACKAGE (6.5 OUNCES) PIZZA CRUST MIX
- ½ TEASPOON DRIED OREGANO LEAVES
- ½ CUP HOT WATER
- ALL-PURPOSE FLOUR
- 1 GARLIC CLOVE
- 1 CAN (8 OUNCES) PIZZA SAUCE

Tools:

MEASURE-ALL® CUP

ADJUSTABLE MEASURING SPOON

MY SAFE CUTTER™

13" X 9" CUTTING BOARD

1-QT. BATTER BOWL

DELUXE CHEESE GRATER

CLASSIC 2-QT. BATTER BOWL WITH LID

BAMBOO SPOON

PIZZA CUTTER

12" X 15" RECTANGLE OR 15" ROUND BAKING STONE WITH OVEN-TO-TABLE RACK

GARLIC PRESS

ALL-PURPOSE SPREADER

OVEN MITTS

CAN OPENER

COVERED MICRO-COOKER®

1 Preheat oven to 425°F. Place butter in **1-Qt. Batter Bowl** and set aside to soften at room temperature.

2 Using **Deluxe Cheese Grater** fitted with fine grating drum, grate Parmesan cheese into **Classic 2-Qt. Batter Bowl**. Stir in pizza crust mix and oregano using **Bamboo Spoon**.

3 Add hot water and stir until moistened. Continue to stir vigorously about 25 strokes. Cover Batter Bowl with lid and let stand 5 minutes in a warm place.

4 Sprinkle a small amount of flour over **Cutting Board** so the dough doesn't stick. Turn dough out onto cutting board and knead the dough 10-12 times (see Cook's Tip). Divide dough into 8 equal pieces using **Pizza Cutter**. Using hands, roll each piece into a 10-inch rope.

5 Shape ropes into letters on **12" x 15" Rectangle** or **15" Round Baking Stone**.

6 Using **Garlic Press**, press garlic over softened butter in Batter Bowl and mix with bamboo spoon. Spread butter mixture over letters using **All-Purpose Spreader**. Place Baking Stone in **Oven-To-Table Rack**.

7 *Adult help:* Bake 11-12 minutes or until golden brown. Using **Oven Mitts**, remove from oven.

8 Pour pizza sauce into **Covered Micro-Cooker®**. Microwave on HIGH 1-1½ minutes or until warm. Serve warm bread sticks with pizza sauce for dipping.

Approximately 110 calories and 5 grams of fat per serving

Cook's Tip:

WHAT DOES "KNEAD" MEAN? TO KNEAD DOUGH, FLATTEN A ROUND BALL OF DOUGH ON A CUTTING BOARD SPRINKLED WITH A LITTLE FLOUR. FOLD THE DOUGH IN HALF TOWARD YOU. WITH THE HEELS OF YOUR HANDS, PUSH DOUGH AWAY FROM YOU IN A ROLLING MOTION. ROTATE DOUGH ONE-QUARTER TURN AND REPEAT THE SAME MOTIONS— GENTLY FOLD-ING, PUSHING AND TURNING.

My "X-Tra" Special Cinnamon Rolls p. 22

Rise 'n Shine!

A warm cinnamon roll and a tall glass of juice...

Life doesn't get much better.

My "X-Tra" Special Cinnamon Rolls

GIVE SOMEONE YOU LOVE A WAKE-UP CALL WITH THESE
HOT-FROM-THE-OVEN CINNAMON ROLLS.

MAKES 8 SERVINGS

Ingredients:

2 PACKAGES (12.4 OUNCES EACH)
   REFRIGERATED CINNAMON ROLLS
   WITH ICING
2 MEDIUM GRANNY SMITH APPLES
3 TABLESPOONS BUTTER OR
   MARGARINE
2 TABLESPOONS SUGAR
1 TEASPOON GROUND CINNAMON

Tools:

ADJUSTABLE MEASURING SPOON
QUIKUT PARING KNIFE
13" X 9" CUTTING BOARD
DEEP DISH BAKER
APPLE PEELER/CORER/SLICER
CLASSIC 2-QT. BATTER BOWL
   WITH LID
SUPER SCRAPER
FLOUR/SUGAR SHAKER
OVEN MITTS
NONSTICK COOLING RACK
ALL-PURPOSE SPREADER
MINI-SERVING SPATULA

1 Preheat oven to 375°F. Set icing aside. Separate rolls into 16 pieces. Place rolls, cinnamon topping side up, in **Deep Dish Baker** (11 around edge and 5 in center).

2 *Adult help:* Peel, core and slice apples using **Apple Peeler/Corer/Slicer** and place on **Cutting Board.** Cut apples crosswise in half with **Quikut Paring Knife.**

3 Place butter in **Classic 2-Qt. Batter Bowl.** Microwave on HIGH 30 seconds or until melted. Add apple slices. Using **Super Scraper,** gently stir until slices are evenly coated with butter.

4 Combine sugar and cinnamon in **Flour/Sugar Shaker** and sprinkle over apples. Cover Batter Bowl with lid and shake until apples are evenly coated. Place an apple slice between each biscuit and around outer edge of Baker.

5 *Adult help:* Bake 30-33 minutes or until top is deep golden brown. Using **Oven Mitts,** remove Baker to **Nonstick Cooling Rack.**

6 Using **All-Purpose Spreader,** spread top of hot rolls with 1 container of icing. (Refrigerate second container of icing to frost graham crackers or for other use.) Serve warm using **Mini-Serving Spatula.**

Approximately 370 calories and 16 grams of fat per serving

Honey Granola Crunch

CRISPY, CRUNCHY AND BETTER THAN STUFF FROM A BOX, YOU'LL LIKE EATING THIS HOMEMADE CEREAL FOR BREAKFAST OR A SNACK.

MAKES 12 SERVINGS (6 CUPS)

Ingredients:

- 1 CUP NUTS
- 4 CUPS QUICK OR OLD-FASHIONED OATS
- ¼ CUP PACKED BROWN SUGAR
- 1½ TEASPOONS GROUND CINNAMON
- ¼ TEASPOON SALT
- ⅓ CUP STICK BUTTER OR MARGARINE
- ¼ CUP HONEY

Tools:

ADJUSTABLE SCOOP

ADJUSTABLE MEASURING SPOONS

MEASURE-ALL® CUP

MY SAFE CUTTER™

FOOD CHOPPER

13" X 9" CUTTING BOARD

9" X 13" BAKER

MIX 'N SCRAPER®

COVERED MICRO-COOKER®

OVEN MITTS

NONSTICK COOLING RACK

1 Preheat oven to 375°F. On **Cutting Board,** coarsely chop nuts, about ¼ cup at a time, using **Food Chopper.**

2 In 9" x 13" **Baker,** mix nuts, oats, brown sugar, cinnamon and salt using **Mix 'N Scraper®.**

3 Place butter in **Covered Micro-Cooker®.** Microwave on HIGH 1 minute or until melted. Stir in honey.

4 Pour butter mixture over oat mixture and stir with scraper until oat mixture is evenly coated.

5 *Adult help:* Bake 25-30 minutes or until golden brown, stirring every 10 minutes so mixture browns evenly. Using **Oven Mitts,** remove Baker to **Nonstick Cooling Rack.** Stir.

6 Cool completely. Store in a tightly covered container.

Approximately 240 calories and 14 grams of fat per serving (½ cup)

Cook's Tips:

IF YOU LIKE, ADD 1 CUP OF YOUR FAVORITE DRIED FRUIT SUCH AS RAISINS, CRANBERRIES, BLUEBERRIES, COCONUT OR CHOPPED DATES TO THE OAT MIXTURE AFTER REMOVING FROM THE OVEN.

FOR A SPEEDY SNACK, SPRINKLE HONEY GRANOLA CRUNCH OVER YOGURT OR CUT-UP FRESH FRUITS OR JUST ENJOY A HANDFUL!

CRUNCHED FOR TIME BUT HUNGRY FOR DESSERT? SPRINKLE HONEY GRANOLA CRUNCH OVER YOUR FAVORITE WARMED FRUIT PIE FILLING AND TOP WITH WHIPPED TOPPING OR ICE CREAM.

FOR AN EXTRA SPECIAL DESSERT, USE HONEY GRANOLA CRUNCH IN OUR STRIPED PUDDING PARFAITS (PAGE 77).

Tex-Mex Breakfast Burritos

Tex-Mex Breakfast Burritos

CHEESY SCRAMBLED EGGS STAY DELICIOUSLY MOIST TUCKED INSIDE A WARM TORTILLA.
TOP WITH SALSA FOR A REAL EYE-OPENER!

MAKES 4 SERVINGS

Ingredients:

- 2 OUNCES CO-JACK CHEESE, SHREDDED (½ CUP)
- 1 GREEN ONION WITH TOP
- 4 (6-7 INCH) FLOUR TORTILLAS
- 4 EGGS
- ¼ CUP MILK
- ⅛ TEASPOON SALT
- DASH OF PEPPER
- 1 TEASPOON BUTTER OR MARGARINE
- 1 TABLESPOON REAL BACON BITS
- ¼ CUP THICK AND CHUNKY SALSA

Tools:

MEASURE-ALL® CUP
ADJUSTABLE MEASURING SPOONS
QUIKUT PARING KNIFE
13" X 9" CUTTING BOARD
DELUXE CHEESE GRATER
KITCHEN SPRITZER
8" MINI-BAKER
MINI-BAKING BOWL
OVEN MITTS
NONSTICK COOLING RACK
1-QT. BATTER BOWL
10" WHISK
GENERATION II 8" OPEN SAUTE PAN
SUPER SCRAPER

1 Preheat oven to 275°F. Shred Co-Jack cheese using **Deluxe Cheese Grater** fitted with coarse shredding drum and set aside.

2 On **Cutting Board**, cut root end off green onion. Thinly slice with **Quikut Paring Knife** and set aside.

3 Lightly spray tortillas with water using **Kitchen Spritzer**. Place in **8" Mini-Baker** and cover with **Mini-Baking Bowl**.

4 *Adult help:* Place Mini-Baker in oven to warm tortillas, about 10 minutes. Using **Oven Mitts**, remove Mini-Baker to **Nonstick Cooling Rack**.

5 Meanwhile, crack eggs into **1-Qt. Batter Bowl**. Add milk, salt and pepper. Mix with **10" Whisk** to combine.

6 In **Generation II 8" Open Saute Pan**, melt butter over medium heat until it starts to bubble. Add egg mixture to pan. Let cook 1 minute without stirring. Stir with **Super Scraper**. Continue cooking 3-4 minutes until eggs are firm but still moist, stirring occasionally. Stir in bacon bits as eggs begin to set. Remove pan from heat.

7 For each burrito, spoon about ⅓ cup of the scrambled egg mixture down the center of 1 tortilla. Top with 2 tablespoons of shredded cheese, a few green onion slices and 1 tablespoon salsa. Fold sides of tortilla over eggs. Serve with extra salsa, if desired.

Approximately 250 calories and 13 grams of fat per serving

Toasty Breakfast Pockets

THESE MINI BREAKFAST SANDWICHES RIVAL THOSE FOUND
AT YOUR FAVORITE FAST FOOD RESTAURANT.

MAKES 6 SERVINGS (12 POCKETS)

Ingredients:

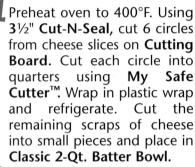

6 SLICES (¾ OUNCE EACH)
   AMERICAN CHEESE

2 HARD-COOKED EGGS, PEELED

2 OUNCES SLICED DELI TURKEY
   BREAST, CHOPPED (½ CUP)

1 TABLESPOON MAYONNAISE

24 SLICES SOFT WHEAT OR
   WHITE BREAD

3 TABLESPOONS BUTTER
   OR MARGARINE

PAPRIKA (IF DESIRED)

Tools:

ADJUSTABLE MEASURING SPOON

MY SAFE CUTTER™

13" X 9" CUTTING BOARD

3½" CUT-N-SEAL

CLASSIC 2-QT. BATTER BOWL

EGG SLICER PLUS®

FOOD CHOPPER

SUPER SCRAPER

SMALL STAINLESS STEEL SCOOP

FLAT BAKING STONE WITH
   OVEN-TO-TABLE RACK

COVERED MICRO-COOKER®

PASTRY BRUSH

OVEN MITTS

NONSTICK COOLING RACK

1 Preheat oven to 400°F. Using 3½" **Cut-N-Seal**, cut 6 circles from cheese slices on **Cutting Board**. Cut each circle into quarters using **My Safe Cutter™**. Wrap in plastic wrap and refrigerate. Cut the remaining scraps of cheese into small pieces and place in **Classic 2-Qt. Batter Bowl**.

2 For each egg, slice egg using **Egg Slicer Plus®**. Turn the egg a quarter turn and slice again to make small pieces. Add egg pieces to Batter Bowl.

3 Using **Food Chopper**, chop turkey. Add turkey and mayonnaise to Batter Bowl. Mix lightly with **Super Scraper.**

4 For each pocket, place one bread slice on cutting board. Gently pat down center of bread. Using small **Stainless Steel Scoop**, place a level scoop of egg mixture in center of bread slice. Gently pat down center of second bread slice and place over filling. Use Cut-N-Seal to make pockets.

5 Arrange pockets on flat **Baking Stone** placed in **Oven-To-Table Rack**. Place butter in **Covered Micro-Cooker®**. Microwave on HIGH 30 seconds or until melted. Using **Pastry Brush**, brush tops of pockets with butter.

6 *Adult help:* Bake 11-12 minutes or until lightly browned. Using **Oven Mitts**, remove Baking Stone to **Nonstick Cooling Rack**. Top each pocket with 2 pieces of cheese and sprinkle with paprika, if desired.

7 *Adult help:* Return Baking Stone to oven and continue baking 1 minute or until cheese begins to melt. Serve warm.

Approximately 410 calories and 17 grams of fat per serving (2 pockets)

Cook's Tip:

TO HARD COOK EGGS, PLACE EGGS IN **GENERATION II 1½-QT. SAUCEPAN** AND FILL WITH ENOUGH COLD WATER TO COVER EGGS. BRING WATER TO A BOIL. REMOVE SAUCEPAN FROM HEAT. COVER AND LET STAND **20** MINUTES. IMMEDIATELY RUN COLD WATER INTO PAN TO COOL EGGS.

Toasty Breakfast Pockets, Deliciously Golden Applesauce p. 28

Deliciously Golden Applesauce

COUNT THIS EASY, HOMEMADE APPLESAUCE AS YOUR APPLE FOR THE DAY. IT'S THE PERFECT COMPLEMENT TO TOASTY BREAKFAST POCKETS OR FRENCH TOAST DIPPERS.

MAKES 6 SERVINGS (3 CUPS)

Ingredients:

6 MEDIUM GOLDEN DELICIOUS
  APPLES (ABOUT 2 POUNDS)
1 CUP APPLE JUICE
1 TABLESPOON FRESH LEMON JUICE

Tools:

MEASURE-ALL® CUP
ADJUSTABLE MEASURING SPOON
APPLE PEELER/CORER/SLICER
13" X 9" CUTTING BOARD
QUIKUT PARING KNIFE
GENERATION II 3-QT. SAUCEPAN
BAMBOO SPOON
OVEN PAD
NYLON MASHER
FLOUR/SUGAR SHAKER
LEMON AID

1 *Adult help:* Peel, core and slice apples using **Apple Peeler/Corer/Slicer** and place apples on **Cutting Board.** Cut apples in half crosswise with **Quikut Paring Knife.**

2 Place apple slices, apple juice and lemon juice in **Generation II 3-Qt. Saucepan** and bring to a boil over medium-high heat. Reduce heat to medium and cook 10 minutes, stirring occasionally with **Bamboo Spoon.**

3 *Adult help:* Remove pan from heat and place on **Oven Pad.** Using **Nylon Masher,** carefully mash apple mixture until it is as smooth as you like it.

4 Let applesauce cool to room temperature. Spoon into air-tight container and store in refrigerator.

Approximately 90 calories and 0 grams of fat per serving (½ cup)

Cook's Tip:

FOR CINNAMON-FLAVORED APPLE-SAUCE, SPRINKLE EACH SERVING WITH GROUND CINNAMON OR COMBINE 1 TABLESPOON SUGAR AND ¼ TEASPOON GROUND CINNAMON IN **FLOUR/SUGAR SHAKER** AND SPRINKLE OVER APPLESAUCE.

Tool Tip:

FOR FRESH LEMON JUICE, ROLL A LEMON FIRMLY BETWEEN THE PALM OF YOUR HAND AND CUTTING BOARD. CUT A THIN SLICE OFF THE STEM END OF LEMON USING QUIKUT PARING KNIFE. PUSH SPOUT FROM **LEMON AID** INTO CUT END OF LEMON BY TWISTING DOWNWARD. OPEN SPOUT LID AND SQUEEZE FOR JUICE.

Dreamy Pudding Pillows

TENDER, FLAKY BISCUITS ARE FILLED WITH
A CREAMY, SWEET SURPRISE!

MAKES 8 SERVINGS

Ingredients:

- 1 PACKAGE (17.3 OUNCES) GRAND-SIZE REFRIGERATED BUTTERMILK BISCUITS
- 2 SNACK-SIZE CUPS (3½ OUNCES EACH) PREPARED VANILLA OR CHOCOLATE PUDDING
- ½ CUP POWDERED SUGAR

Tools:

ADJUSTABLE SCOOP

13" ROUND BAKING STONE WITH OVEN-TO-TABLE RACK

OVEN MITTS

NONSTICK COOLING RACK

EASY ACCENT® DECORATOR

ALL-PURPOSE SPREADER

1 Preheat oven to 375°F. Place biscuits 1-2 inches apart on **13" Round Baking Stone.** Place Baking Stone in **Oven-To-Table Rack.**

2 *Adult help:* Bake 11-15 minutes or until golden brown. Using **Oven Mitts,** remove Baking Stone to **Nonstick Cooling Rack.**

3 Meanwhile, attach **Bismark Tip** to **Easy Accent® Decorator** and fill tube with pudding.

4 Place powdered sugar in large resealable plastic bag. Place 1 biscuit in bag. Seal bag and shake until biscuit is heavily coated with powdered sugar. Remove biscuit from bag and place on Nonstick Cooling Rack. Repeat with remaining biscuits.

5 For each biscuit, gently insert full length of Bismark Tip into side of biscuit. Push down trigger to squeeze pudding into biscuit just until center of biscuit begins to rise. Serve warm or at room temperature. Refrigerate leftovers.

Approximately 260 calories and 11 grams of fat per serving

Boston Creme Biscuits:
Leave out the powdered sugar. Let baked biscuits cool to room temperature. Use **All-Purpose Spreader** to frost tops of biscuits with prepared chocolate frosting. Fill with vanilla pudding.

Fabulous Frosty Fruit

Fabulous Frosty Fruit

WHO SAYS BREAKFAST IS BORING? START THE DAY
OUT RIGHT WITH FUN, FRUITY FARE!

MAKES 8 SERVINGS

Ingredients:

I CAN (8½ OUNCES) SLICED
PEACHES IN SYRUP

I CAN (11.5 OUNCES) PEACH NECTAR

I PACKAGE (10 OUNCES) FROZEN
SLICED STRAWBERRIES IN SYRUP,
THAWED

I MEDIUM CANTALOUPE

Tools:

CAN OPENER

I-QT. BATTER BOWL

FOOD CHOPPER

13" X 9" CUTTING BOARD

BAMBOO SPOON

ICE SHAVER WITH TUBS

CHILLZANNE® MINI-BOWL

GARNISHER OR CRINKLE CUTTER

MEDIUM STAINLESS STEEL SCOOP

1 Place a colander over **1-Qt. Batter Bowl.** Drain peaches in colander, reserving syrup in Batter Bowl.

2 On **Cutting Board**, finely chop peaches using **Food Chopper.** Add chopped peaches, nectar and strawberries to Batter Bowl. Stir with **Bamboo Spoon.**

3 Divide mixture evenly among 3 **Ice Shaver Tubs** and cover with lids. Place tubs and **Chillzanne® Mini-Bowl** in freezer. Freeze mixture until firm (about 6 hours).

4 *Adult help:* When ready to serve, prepare cantaloupe wedges before shaving fruit mixture. Using **Garnisher** or **Crinkle Cutter**, cut cantaloupe in half through the middle on cutting board. Scoop out seeds. Starting with one melon half, use Garnisher to cut melon evenly into 4 small wedges. Repeat with other melon half to make a total of 8 wedges.

5 Place Chillzanne® Mini-Bowl under **Ice Shaver** to catch shavings. Remove frozen mixture from 1 tub and shave with Ice Shaver.

6 Using medium **Stainless Steel Scoop**, place 1 scoop of shaved fruit mixture in each cantaloupe wedge. Serve immediately. Save the 2 remaining tubs of frozen fruit mixture to make this breakfast treat again or to enjoy for a snack or dessert.

Approximately 45 calories and 0 grams of fat per serving (1 scoop shaved fruit mixture and ⅛ cantaloupe)

Cook's Tip:

TO CHOOSE A GOOD CANTALOUPE, FIRST LOOK FOR A MELON WITH THICK, CREAM-COLORED NETTING OVER THE SURFACE. IT SHOULD FEEL HEAVY FOR ITS SIZE. PRESS ON THE BLOSSOM END TO SEE IF IT WILL GIVE SLIGHTLY AND CHECK IF THE MELON SMELLS SWEET. ONLY REFRIGERATE A MELON ONCE IT IS RIPE.

Hot Griddle Cakes

IT'S THE WEEKEND AND THE PERFECT TIME TO GATHER AROUND
THE TABLE FOR EVERYONE'S FAVORITE BREAKFAST!

MAKES 4 SERVINGS (12-14 PANCAKES)

Ingredients:

1 MEDIUM APPLE
1½ CUPS COMPLETE BUTTERMILK
    PANCAKE MIX
½ CUP QUICK OATS (NOT INSTANT)
½ TEASPOON GROUND CINNAMON
1½ CUPS WATER
    VEGETABLE OIL

Tools:

ADJUSTABLE SCOOP
ADJUSTABLE MEASURING SPOON
APPLE PEELER/CORER/SLICER
13" X 9" CUTTING BOARD
QUIKUT PARING KNIFE
FOOD CHOPPER
CLASSIC 2-QT. BATTER BOWL
10" WHISK
GENERATION II 11" SQUARE GRIDDLE
KITCHEN SPRITZER
NYLON SPATULA
NYLON MASHER

1 *Adult help:* Peel, core and slice apple using **Apple Peeler/Corer/Slicer** and place apple on **Cutting Board.** Cut apple in quarters with **Quikut Paring Knife.** Chop apple pieces, a few at a time, using **Food Chopper.**

2 In **Classic 2-Qt. Batter Bowl,** combine pancake mix, oats and cinnamon. Add water and stir with **10" Whisk** just until the large lumps disappear. (The batter should have small lumps.) Stir in chopped apple.

3 Lightly spray **Generation II 11" Square Griddle** with vegetable oil using **Kitchen Spritzer.** Heat griddle over medium heat until hot. (Sprinkle griddle with a few drops of water. When the drops sizzle and then disappear, it's ready for cooking.)

4 For each pancake, pour about ¼ cup batter onto griddle. (You'll be able to cook 4 pancakes at a time.) Cook until bubbles appear on the surfaces and edges look cooked. Turn pancakes over with **Nylon Spatula** and cook until golden brown on bottoms.

Approximately 360 calories and 10 grams of fat per serving

Banana Griddle Cakes:
Leave out the apple and oats. Use 2 cups pancake mix. Mash 1 medium banana with **Nylon Masher.** Add mashed banana to the batter and prepare pancakes as directed.

Cook's Tips:

FOR TENDER, FLUFFY PANCAKES BE CAREFUL NOT TO OVERMIX THE BATTER. BESIDES, THOSE LITTLE LUMPS WILL DISAPPEAR WHILE THE PANCAKES COOK.

PATIENCE…PATIENCE. TURN PANCAKES ONLY ONCE OR YOU'LL GET TOUGH RESULTS.

FOR THICKER PANCAKES, YOU CAN USE A LITTLE LESS WATER. FOR THINNER PANCAKES, USE A LITTLE MORE WATER.

Hot Griddle Cakes

Early Risin' Raisin Scones

EVEN SLEEPYHEADS WON'T BE ABLE TO RESIST THE SWEET SMELL OF THESE FRESHLY BAKED BREAKFAST BISCUITS!

MAKES 8 SERVINGS

Ingredients:

SCONES

2½ CUPS ALL-PURPOSE BAKING MIX

½ CUP RAISINS

⅓ CUP MILK

2 TABLESPOONS SUGAR

2 TABLESPOONS BUTTER OR MARGARINE, MELTED

I EGG

TOPPING

I TABLESPOON SUGAR

⅛ TEASPOON GROUND CINNAMON

Tools:

ADJUSTABLE SCOOP

MEASURE-ALL® CUP

ADJUSTABLE MEASURING SPOONS

MY SAFE CUTTER™

13" X 9" CUTTING BOARD

CLASSIC 2-QT. BATTER BOWL

MIX 'N SCRAPER®

13" ROUND BAKING STONE WITH OVEN-TO-TABLE RACK

DOUGH AND PIZZA ROLLER

PIZZA CUTTER

FLOUR/SUGAR SHAKER

OVEN MITTS

NONSTICK COOLING RACK

1 Preheat oven to 425°F. For scones, in **Classic 2-Qt. Batter Bowl**, mix baking mix, raisins, milk, 2 tablespoons sugar, melted butter and egg with **Mix 'N Scraper®** until all the ingredients are moistened and a soft dough forms.

2 Sprinkle a little extra baking mix over **Cutting Board** so the dough doesn't stick. Turn dough out onto cutting board and lightly knead the dough 8-10 times (see Cook's Tip).

3 Place dough in center of **13" Round Baking Stone**. Using **Dough and Pizza Roller**, lightly sprinkled with baking mix, roll the dough into a 9-inch circle, about ½ inch thick. Using **Pizza Cutter**, cut dough into 8 wedges, but do not separate from circle.

4 For the topping, combine the remaining 1 tablespoon sugar and cinnamon in **Flour/Sugar Shaker**. Sprinkle over dough. Place Baking Stone in **Oven-To-Table Rack**.

5 *Adult help:* Bake 12-13 minutes or until light golden brown. Using **Oven Mitts**, remove Baking Stone to **Nonstick Cooling Rack**. Using Pizza Cutter, cut through dough along original lines to separate scones.

6 Serve warm scones with butter, honey or jam, if desired.

Approximately 290 calories and 11 grams of fat per serving

Cook's Tips:

WHAT DOES "KNEAD" MEAN? TO KNEAD DOUGH, FLATTEN A ROUND BALL OF DOUGH ON A CUTTING BOARD SPRINKLED WITH A LITTLE FLOUR. FOLD THE DOUGH IN HALF TOWARD YOU. WITH THE HEELS OF YOUR HANDS, PUSH DOUGH AWAY FROM YOU IN A ROLLING MOTION. ROTATE DOUGH ONE-QUARTER TURN AND REPEAT THE SAME MOTIONS— GENTLY FOLDING, PUSHING AND TURNING.

SCONES ARE JUST FANCY BISCUITS WITH A NEAT NAME. ORIGINATING IN SCOTLAND, SCONES ARE SWEETER AND RICHER THAN REGULAR BISCUITS AND THEY USUALLY HAVE DRIED FRUIT OR NUTS IN THEM.

French Toast Dippers

GO AHEAD — USE YOUR FINGERS. THE SECRET TO THESE DELICIOUS
FRENCH TOAST STICKS IS THE CRISPY CEREAL COATING.

MAKES 4 SERVINGS

Ingredients:

4-5 SLICES WHITE BREAD

3 CUPS CRISPY RICE CEREAL

1 TABLESPOON SUGAR

¾ TEASPOON GROUND CINNAMON

3 EGGS

½ CUP MILK

1 TEASPOON VANILLA

⅛ TEASPOON SALT

2 TABLESPOONS BUTTER OR MARGARINE

MAPLE SYRUP OR DELICIOUSLY GOLDEN APPLESAUCE (PAGE 28)

Tools:

ADJUSTABLE SCOOP

MEASURE-ALL® CUP

ADJUSTABLE MEASURING SPOONS

QUIKUT PARING KNIFE

13" X 9" CUTTING BOARD

PIZZA CUTTER

NONSTICK COOLING RACK

DOUGH AND PIZZA ROLLER

BAMBOO SPOON

STONEWARE 9" PIE PLATE

CLASSIC 2-QT. BATTER BOWL

10" WHISK

9" X 13" BAKER

COVERED MICRO-COOKER®

OVEN MITTS

1 On **Cutting Board,** cut each bread slice crosswise into 4 sticks using **Pizza Cutter.** Place bread on **Nonstick Cooling Rack** for about 20 minutes to dry out slightly.

2 Preheat oven to 425°F. Place cereal in a resealable plastic bag and crush to fine crumbs using **Dough and Pizza Roller.** Pour crumbs into **Stoneware 9" Pie Plate** and add sugar and cinnamon. Mix with **Bamboo Spoon** and set aside.

3 In **Classic 2-Qt. Batter Bowl,** mix eggs, milk, vanilla and salt with **10" Whisk.**

4 Dip 1 bread stick at a time into egg mixture and then roll in crumb mixture. Place in **9" x 13" Baker.**

5 Place butter in **Covered Micro-Cooker®.** Microwave on HIGH 30 seconds or until melted. Slowly pour butter over bread sticks.

6 *Adult help:* Bake 17-19 minutes or until hot and crispy. Using **Oven Mitts,** remove Baker to cooling rack.

7 Fill small cups with syrup or applesauce for dipping and serve with French Toast Dippers.

Approximately 330 calories and 12 grams of fat per serving (4 sticks)

Cook's Tip:

MAKING FRENCH TOAST DIPPERS IS THE PERFECT WAY TO USE UP BREAD THAT ISN'T FRESH ENOUGH FOR SANDWICHES ANYMORE.

Taco Grande p. 38

What's for Dinner?

Go ahead, impress your family.

Dinner's going to be great!

Taco Grande

THIS IS ONE GIANT TACO! LAYER ALL YOUR FAVORITE TACO FIXINGS BETWEEN
SOFT FLOUR TORTILLAS AND BAKE UNTIL HOT AND BUBBLY.

MAKES 8 SERVINGS

Ingredients: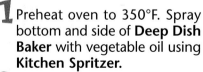

- 1 POUND GROUND TURKEY
- 1 PACKAGE (1 OUNCE) TACO SEASONING MIX
- WATER
- 1 JAR (16 OUNCES) SALSA
- 8 (6-7 INCH) FLOUR TORTILLAS
- 2 CUPS (8 OUNCES) SHREDDED CO-JACK CHEESE
- 1 GREEN ONION
- 4 CUPS SHREDDED ICEBERG LETTUCE
- ½ CUP SOUR CREAM

Tools:

- ADJUSTABLE SCOOP
- MEASURE-ALL® CUP
- DEEP DISH BAKER
- KITCHEN SPRITZER
- GENERATION II 10" FRYING PAN
- BAMBOO SPOON
- QUIKUT PARING KNIFE
- 13" X 9" CUTTING BOARD
- SKINNY SCRAPER
- OVEN MITTS
- OVEN PAD
- SLICE 'N SERVE®
- GARNISHER OR CRINKLE CUTTER

1 Preheat oven to 350°F. Spray bottom and side of **Deep Dish Baker** with vegetable oil using **Kitchen Spritzer.**

2 Place turkey in **Generation II 10" Frying Pan.** Cook and stir over medium heat 8-10 minutes or until turkey is no longer pink, breaking turkey into small crumbles using **Bamboo Spoon.**

3 Add taco mix and amount of water directed on package. Continue cooking according to package directions. Remove pan from heat. Stir in 1 cup of the salsa.

4 Arrange 4 tortillas in bottom and up side of Baker. (Tortillas will overlap on bottom of Baker but not all of the area on the side of the Baker will be covered.)

5 Spoon turkey mixture evenly over tortillas. Sprinkle with 1 cup of the cheese. Slice green onion with **Quikut Paring Knife** on **Cutting Board.** Sprinkle half of the onion over cheese.

6 Top with remaining 4 tortillas, overlapping tortillas slightly to create a scalloped edge effect. Press tortillas down over filling. Spread remaining salsa over tortillas using **Skinny Scraper.** Sprinkle with remaining cheese and onion.

7 *Adult help:* Bake 30 minutes. Using **Oven Mitts,** remove Baker to **Oven Pad.** Let stand 5 minutes. Cut into wedges using **Slice 'N Serve®.**

8 Using **Garnisher** or **Crinkle Cutter,** chop lettuce into thin strands. Serve taco wedges over lettuce and top with sour cream.

Approximately 360 calories and 19 grams of fat per serving

The Easiest Kid-Pleasin' Lasagna Ever

NEED WE SAY MORE? OH, BY THE WAY— YOU DON'T HAVE TO COOK THE LASAGNA NOODLES AHEAD OF TIME. HOW DO YOU LIKE THAT FOR EASE?

MAKES 12 SERVINGS

Ingredients:

- 1 JAR (26-28 OUNCES) SPAGHETTI SAUCE
- 1 CAN (14½ OUNCES) DICED TOMATOES WITH BASIL, GARLIC & OREGANO (DO NOT DRAIN)
- ½ CUP WATER
- 1 OUNCE FRESH PARMESAN CHEESE, GRATED (¼ CUP)
- ¼ CUP SNIPPED FRESH PARSLEY
- 1 EGG
- 1 CARTON (15 OUNCES) PART-SKIM RICOTTA CHEESE
- 10 UNCOOKED LASAGNA NOODLES
- 3 CUPS (12 OUNCES) SHREDDED MOZZARELLA CHEESE

Tools:

MEASURE-ALL® CUP
ADJUSTABLE SCOOP
CAN OPENER
KITCHEN SHEARS
CLASSIC 2-QT. BATTER BOWL
MIX 'N SCRAPER®
DELUXE CHEESE GRATER
1-QT. BATTER BOWL
10" WHISK
9" X 13" BAKER
ALL-PURPOSE SPREADER
OVEN MITTS
STONEWARE TRIVET

1 Preheat oven to 400°F. In **Classic 2-Qt. Batter Bowl**, combine spaghetti sauce, undrained tomatoes and water with **Mix 'N Scraper®** and set aside.

2 Using **Deluxe Cheese Grater** fitted with fine grating drum, grate Parmesan cheese. Place parsley in a small, deep bowl and snip using **Kitchen Shears.**

3 In **1-Qt. Batter Bowl,** mix egg with **10" Whisk.** Add ricotta cheese, Parmesan cheese and parsley and mix well with scraper.

4 To assemble lasagna, spread 1½ cups of the sauce over bottom of **9" x 13" Baker.**

5 Arrange 5 of the uncooked noodles in single layer over sauce by placing 4 noodles lengthwise and 1 noodle crosswise to cover bottom of Baker. (Break off and discard ends of noodles, if necessary, so that noodles will fit flat in the Baker.) Press noodles into sauce.

6 Spread all of the ricotta cheese mixture over noodles using **All-Purpose Spreader.** Sprinkle with half (1½ cups) of the mozzarella cheese.

7 Top with 1½ cups of the sauce and remaining 5 uncooked noodles, breaking noodles to fit. Press noodles into sauce. Spread the remaining sauce over noodles. Cover Baker with aluminum foil. (At this point, lasagna can be refrigerated for several hours or overnight.)

8 *Adult help:* Bake 45 minutes (55 minutes if lasagna was refrigerated) or until noodles are tender. Using **Oven Mitts,** remove Baker to **Stoneware Trivet.** Uncover carefully and sprinkle with remaining mozzarella cheese. Cover loosely with foil; let stand 15 minutes. Cut into squares.

Approximately 260 calories and 12 grams of fat per serving

Bacon 'N Cheddar Bubble Bread

Bacon 'N Cheddar Bubble Bread

THIS PULL-APART DINNER LOAF IS AS MUCH
FUN TO MAKE AS IT IS TO EAT.

MAKES 8 SERVINGS

Ingredients:

1 PACKAGE (11 OUNCES)
    REFRIGERATED DINNER ROLLS
2 OUNCES CHEDDAR CHEESE, FINELY
    SHREDDED (½ CUP)
1 TABLESPOON REAL BACON BITS

Tools:

QUIKUT PARING KNIFE
13" X 9" CUTTING BOARD
ADJUSTABLE SCOOP
ADJUSTABLE MEASURING SPOON
8" MINI-BAKER
KITCHEN SPRITZER
KITCHEN SHEARS
DELUXE CHEESE GRATER
1-QT. BATTER BOWL
OVEN MITTS
NONSTICK COOLING RACK
MINI-SERVING SPATULA

1 Preheat oven to 375°F. Lightly spray **8" Mini-Baker** with vegetable oil using **Kitchen Spritzer.**

2 On **Cutting Board**, separate dough into 8 rolls. Using **Kitchen Shears**, cut each roll into quarters.

3 Using **Deluxe Cheese Grater** fitted with fine grating drum, finely shred cheese into **1-Qt. Batter Bowl.** Add bacon bits and mix lightly.

4 Toss each piece of dough in cheese mixture until lightly coated and place in Mini-Baker.

5 *Adult help:* Bake 20-22 minutes or until top is deep golden brown. Using **Oven Mitts**, remove Mini-Baker to **Nonstick Cooling Rack.** Run **Quikut Paring Knife** around edge of bread to loosen. Lift bread onto serving plate with **Mini-Serving Spatula.**

6 To serve, pull apart pieces of rolls from bread loaf.

Approximately 140 calories and 5 grams of fat per serving

Dill 'N Cheddar Bubble Bread: Use 1 teaspoon dried dill weed instead of bacon bits and prepare recipe as directed.

Cook's Tip:

REAL BACON BITS COME PACKAGED IN SMALL CANS OR JARS AND ARE USUALLY FOUND IN THE SUPERMARKET AISLE WITH SALAD DRESSINGS OR CONDIMENTS. IF YOU LIKE, YOU CAN USE 1 BACON SLICE, CRISPLY COOKED AND FINELY CRUMBLED, INSTEAD OF THE REAL BACON BITS.

Cheesy Dogs and Spuds

ONE POTATO, TWO POTATO, THREE POTATO, FOUR...PLUS A FEW MORE INGREDIENTS
IS ALL YOU NEED TO MAKE THIS EASY ONE-DISH MEAL.

MAKES 4 SERVINGS

Ingredients:

¼ CUP CHOPPED ONION

1 CAN (10¾ OUNCES) CONDENSED CHEDDAR CHEESE SOUP

½ CUP MILK

1 TEASPOON PREPARED YELLOW MUSTARD

4 MEDIUM BAKING POTATOES, SCRUBBED (ABOUT 1½ POUNDS)

5 FRANKFURTERS (½ POUND)

1½ CUPS FROZEN CUT GREEN BEANS

1 OUNCE CHEDDAR CHEESE, SHREDDED (¼ CUP)

Tools:

ADJUSTABLE SCOOP

MEASURE-ALL® CUP

ADJUSTABLE MEASURING SPOON

13" X 9" CUTTING BOARD

QUIKUT PARING KNIFE

FOOD CHOPPER

CAN OPENER

1-QT. BATTER BOWL

MIX 'N SCRAPER®

APPLE PEELER/CORER/SLICER

CLASSIC 2-QT. BATTER BOWL

GARNISHER OR CRINKLE CUTTER

9" SQUARE BAKER

OVEN MITTS

OVEN PAD

DELUXE CHEESE GRATER

1 Preheat oven to 375°F. On **Cutting Board,** cut onion into small chunks using **Quikut Paring Knife** then chop using **Food Chopper.** In **1-Qt. Batter Bowl,** mix onion, soup, milk and mustard with **Mix 'N Scraper®** and set aside.

2 *Adult help:* Using **Apple Peeler/Corer/Slicer,** peel, core and slice potatoes. For each potato, coil potato "spiral" back to a stack then cut in half using Quikut Paring Knife. Slice potato "cores" into ¼-inch rounds. Place potatoes in **Classic 2-Qt. Batter Bowl.**

3 Using **Garnisher** or **Crinkle Cutter,** cut frankfurters diagonally into ½-inch- thick slices. Add frankfurters and frozen beans to potatoes.

4 Pour soup mixture over potato mixture and mix well with scraper. Spread mixture evenly in **9" Square Baker** and cover with aluminum foil.

5 *Adult help:* Bake 50 minutes. Using **Oven Mitts,** remove Baker to **Oven Pad.** Let stand, covered, 5 minutes. Carefully remove foil.

6 Using **Deluxe Cheese Grater** fitted with coarse shredding drum, shred cheese over casserole.

Approximately 490 calories and 26 grams of fat per serving

Home On The Range Chili

THERE'S NOTHIN' LIKE A STEAMIN' BOWL
OF RED TO WARM THE SOUL!

MAKES 6 SERVINGS

Ingredients:

- 1 SMALL ONION
- 1 SMALL GREEN BELL PEPPER
- 1 POUND GROUND BEEF
- 1 GARLIC CLOVE
- 1 CAN (14½ OUNCES) DICED TOMATOES (DO NOT DRAIN)
- 1 CAN (8 OUNCES) TOMATO SAUCE
- 2-3 TEASPOONS CHILI POWDER
- ½ TEASPOON SALT
- CRUSHED NACHO CHIPS, SHREDDED CHEDDAR CHEESE OR SOUR CREAM (IF DESIRED)

Tools:

- ADJUSTABLE SCOOP
- ADJUSTABLE MEASURING SPOON
- 13" X 9" CUTTING BOARD
- QUIKUT PARING KNIFE
- FOOD CHOPPER
- CAN OPENER
- GENERATION II 4-QT. CASSEROLE
- GARLIC PRESS
- BAMBOO SPOON
- DELUXE CHEESE GRATER

1 On **Cutting Board**, cut onion and bell pepper into small chunks using **Quikut Paring Knife** then chop using **Food Chopper**.

2 *Adult help:* Place ground beef, onion and bell pepper in **Generation II 4-Qt. Casserole**. Press garlic over beef using **Garlic Press**. Cook over medium heat 8-10 minutes or until beef is no longer pink, breaking beef into small crumbles using **Bamboo Spoon**. Drain off drippings and return beef mixture to Casserole.

3 Stir in tomatoes, tomato sauce, chili powder and salt. Bring mixture to a boil; reduce heat to low. Cover and simmer 30 minutes.

4 Spoon chili into individual serving bowls. Top with crushed nacho chips, shredded cheese or sour cream, if desired.

Approximately 240 calories and 14 grams of fat per serving (1 cup)

Cook's Tips:

USE 2 TEASPOONS CHILI POWDER FOR A MILD CHILI OR 3 TEASPOONS CHILI POWDER FOR A SPICIER ONE.

OTHER TASTY TOPPERS FOR CHILI ARE SLICED GREEN ONIONS, SLICED RIPE OLIVES, OYSTER CRACKERS OR CHEESE-FLAVORED FISH CRACKERS.

Tool Tip:

USE THE **DELUXE CHEESE GRATER** FITTED WITH THE COARSE SHREDDING DRUM FOR SHREDDING CHEDDAR CHEESE OVER INDIVIDUAL SERVINGS OF CHILI, IF DESIRED. ANY EXTRA CHEESE THAT YOU SHRED CAN BE STORED IN THE REFRIGERATOR IN THE **GRATE & STORE™**.

Super Sub

PERFECT FOR AN OUTDOOR PICNIC, THIS GIANT SANDWICH
WILL SATISFY THE BIGGEST APPETITES.

MAKES 8 SERVINGS

Ingredients:

2 PACKAGES (11 OUNCES EACH)
   REFRIGERATED FRENCH BREAD
   DOUGH

⅓ CUP MAYONNAISE

2 TABLESPOONS SWEET PICKLE
   RELISH

½ TEASPOON PREPARED YELLOW
   MUSTARD

1½ CUPS SHREDDED ICEBERG LETTUCE

1 MEDIUM TOMATO

4 OUNCES THINLY SLICED
   AMERICAN CHEESE

8 OUNCES THINLY SLICED DELI
   MEAT SUCH AS: BOLOGNA, HAM
   OR TURKEY

Tools:

MEASURE-ALL® CUP

ADJUSTABLE MEASURING SPOONS

13" ROUND BAKING STONE WITH
   OVEN-TO-TABLE RACK

ALL-PURPOSE SPREADER

OVEN MITTS

OVEN PAD

NONSTICK COOLING RACK

SERRATED BREAD KNIFE

1-QT. BATTER BOWL

SKINNY SCRAPER

GARNISHER OR CRINKLE CUTTER

13" X 9" CUTTING BOARD

TOMATO CORER

QUIKUT PARING KNIFE

FOOD CHOPPER

1 Preheat oven to 350°F. Place bread dough, seam side down, on **13" Round Baking Stone**. Join ends of dough together to form 1 large circle and pinch ends together to seal. Using serrated edge of **All-Purpose Spreader**, cut 6-8 diagonal slashes (½ inch deep) on top of dough. Place Baking Stone in **Oven-To-Table Rack**.

2 *Adult help:* Bake 26-30 minutes or until deep golden brown. Using **Oven Mitts**, remove Baking Stone to **Oven Pad**. Remove bread to **Nonstick Cooling Rack** and cool completely. Cut bread loaf in half horizontally using **Serrated Bread Knife**.

3 In **1-Qt. Batter Bowl**, mix mayonnaise, pickle relish and mustard with **Skinny Scraper** until well blended.

4 On **Cutting Board**, cut lettuce into thin strands using **Garnisher** or **Crinkle Cutter**. Remove stem end of tomato with **Tomato Corer**. Cut into small chunks with **Quikut Paring Knife** then coarsely chop using **Food Chopper**. Cut cheese slices in half diagonally using Garnisher.

5 To assemble the sandwich, spread mayonnaise mixture evenly over the cut side of the bottom half of the bread. Top with lettuce and tomato. Arrange meat and cheese over lettuce and tomato. Cover with top half of bread. Cut into wedges to serve.

Approximately 370 calories and 17 grams of fat per serving

Cook's Tip:

THIS IS A GREAT MIX AND MATCH RECIPE. OTHER CHEESES, SUCH AS CHEDDAR, SWISS AND MUENSTER, AND OTHER MEATS, SUCH AS SALAMI, ROAST BEEF AND CORNED BEEF CAN BE USED. OTHER FRESH VEGGIES CAN BE ADDED TOO—GREEN OR RED BELL PEPPER, ONION, CUCUMBER OR ALFALFA SPROUTS. THE POSSIBILITIES ARE ENDLESS!

Super Sub, Bow Tie Pasta Salad p. 46

Bow Tie Pasta Salad

THERE'S NO SPECIAL DRESS CODE REQUIRED TO
MAKE OR EAT THIS FRESH, FLAVORFUL SALAD!

MAKES 8 SERVINGS

Ingredients:

I TEASPOON DIJON MUSTARD

½ TEASPOON DRIED BASIL LEAVES

⅓ CUP PREPARED ITALIAN SALAD
DRESSING

3 CUPS (6 OUNCES) BOW TIE
(FARFALLE) PASTA, UNCOOKED

20 PITTED RIPE OLIVES

16 CHERRY TOMATOES

I MEDIUM CUCUMBER

I OUNCE FRESH PARMESAN
CHEESE, GRATED (¼ CUP)

SALT AND GROUND BLACK
PEPPER (IF DESIRED)

Tools:

ADJUSTABLE MEASURING SPOON

MEASURE-ALL® CUP

ADJUSTABLE SCOOP

SKINNY SCRAPER

I-QT. BATTER BOWL

10" WHISK

GENERATION II 4-QT. CASSEROLE

CLASSIC 2-QT. BATTER BOWL
WITH LID

13" X 9" CUTTING BOARD

QUIKUT PARING KNIFE

THE CORER™

LEMON ZESTER/SCORER

BAMBOO SPOON

DELUXE CHEESE GRATER

1 In **1-Qt. Batter Bowl**, mix mustard and basil with **10" Whisk**. Gradually stir in dressing and whisk until smooth. Set aside.

2 *Adult help:* In **Generation II 4-Qt. Casserole**, cook pasta according to package directions; drain in colander. Rinse with cold water and drain well. Place pasta in **Classic 2-Qt. Batter Bowl**.

3 While pasta is cooking, prepare the vegetables. On **Cutting Board**, cut olives and cherry tomatoes in half with **Quikut Paring Knife**.

4 *Adult help:* Cut cucumber in half lengthwise. Remove seeds by running **The Corer™** down length of each cucumber half. Place cucumber halves, cut side down, on cutting board. Using scoring hole of **Lemon Zester/Scorer**, remove thin strips of peel to create a striped effect. Cut cucumber halves crosswise into slices.

5 Add olives, cherry tomatoes and cucumbers to pasta in Batter Bowl. Pour dressing over pasta mixture and mix lightly with **Bamboo Spoon**.

6 Using **Deluxe Cheese Grater** fitted with fine grating drum, grate Parmesan cheese over salad and mix lightly. Cover Bowl with lid and refrigerate 30-60 minutes. Before serving, sprinkle salad with a little salt and pepper, if desired.

Approximately 100 calories and 5 grams of fat per serving

Cook's Tip:

TO GET THE MOST FLAVOR FROM YOUR DRIED BASIL LEAVES, CRUSH THE LEAVES IN THE PALM OF YOUR HAND WITH YOUR FINGERTIPS BEFORE YOU MIX THEM WITH THE MUSTARD.

Cheeseburger Pizza

WITH ALL THE FLAVORS OF YOUR FAVORITE FAST-FOOD SANDWICH, YOU'LL LOVE THIS PIZZA!

MAKES 4 SERVINGS

Ingredients:

¼ CUP CHOPPED ONION

½ POUND GROUND BEEF

½ CUP PIZZA SAUCE

1 PACKAGE (6½ OUNCES) PIZZA CRUST MIX

½ CUP HOT WATER

ALL-PURPOSE FLOUR

1 TABLESPOON CORNMEAL

½ CUP DILL OR SWEET PICKLE SLICES (ABOUT 20 SLICES)

2 OUNCES CHEDDAR CHEESE, SHREDDED (½ CUP)

2 OUNCES MOZZARELLA CHEESE, SHREDDED (½ CUP)

Tools:

ADJUSTABLE SCOOP

MEASURE-ALL® CUP

13" X 9" CUTTING BOARD

QUIKUT PARING KNIFE

FOOD CHOPPER

GENERATION II 10" FRYING PAN

BAMBOO SPOON

CLASSIC 2-QT. BATTER BOWL WITH LID

13" ROUND BAKING STONE WITH OVEN-TO-TABLE RACK

DOUGH AND PIZZA ROLLER

DELUXE CHEESE GRATER

OVEN MITTS

PIZZA CUTTER

1 Preheat oven to 400°F. On **Cutting Board,** cut onion into small chunks using **Quikut Paring Knife** then coarsely chop using **Food Chopper.**

2 *Adult help:* Place ground beef and onion in **Generation II 10" Frying Pan.** Cook over medium heat 8-10 minutes or until beef is no longer pink, breaking beef into small crumbles using **Bamboo Spoon.** Drain off drippings and return to frying pan. Stir in pizza sauce.

3 In **Classic 2-Qt. Batter Bowl,** combine pizza crust mix and hot water. Stir with Bamboo Spoon until moistened. Continue to stir vigorously about 25 strokes. Cover with lid and let stand 5 minutes in a warm place. Sprinkle a small amount of flour over cutting board and knead the dough 10-12 times or until dough is smooth (see Cook's Tip, page 19).

4 Sprinkle cornmeal over **13" Round Baking Stone.** Place dough in center of Baking Stone. Using **Dough and Pizza Roller,** lightly sprinkled with flour, roll dough into 12-inch circle.

5 Spread beef mixture over dough to within ¼ inch of edge; top evenly with pickle slices.

6 Using **Deluxe Cheese Grater** fitted with coarse shredding drum, shred cheeses evenly over pizza. Place Baking Stone in **Oven-To-Table Rack.**

7 *Adult help:* Bake on bottom rack of oven 18-20 minutes or until crust is golden brown. Using **Oven Mitts,** remove from oven. Cut into wedges using **Pizza Cutter.**

Approximately 440 calories and 19 grams of fat per serving

Pepperoni Pizza:

Leave out the onion and ground beef. Spread pizza sauce over dough. Top with 20 pepperoni slices instead of the pickles. Sprinkle with cheeses and bake as directed.

Sweetie Potato Pie

OUR EASY ACCENT® DECORATOR MAKES EATING VEGETABLES MORE FUN THAN EVER.

MAKES 6 SERVINGS

Ingredients:

1 CAN (40 OUNCES) CUT SWEET POTATOES IN LIGHT SYRUP
3/4 TEASPOON GROUND CINNAMON
1/4 TEASPOON SALT
15 REGULAR-SIZE MARSHMALLOWS

Tools:

ADJUSTABLE MEASURING SPOON
CAN OPENER
CLASSIC 2-QT. BATTER BOWL
NYLON MASHER
MEDIUM STAINLESS STEEL SCOOP
EASY ACCENT® DECORATOR
STONEWARE 9" PIE PLATE
OVEN MITTS
OVEN PAD

1 Preheat oven to 350°F. Drain sweet potatoes in colander; discard syrup. Place potatoes in **Classic 2-Qt. Batter Bowl.**

2 Sprinkle cinnamon and salt over potatoes. Mash until smooth using **Nylon Masher.**

3 Attach **Open Star Tip** to **Easy Accent® Decorator.** Using medium **Stainless Steel Scoop,** scoop potatoes into tube. (Not all of the potatoes will fit in the beginning.)

4 In **Stoneware 9" Pie Plate,** hold decorator straight up and down with tip about 1 inch above center of plate. Gently squeeze down trigger to form a star. Stop pressure and pull decorator up. Continue to fill the pie plate with potato "stars" until all potatoes are used. Refill decorator as needed.

5 Place marshmallows on their sides around edge of pie plate, on top of potatoes.

6 *Adult help:* Bake 14-16 minutes or until potatoes are heated through and marshmallows are puffed and toasty brown. Using **Oven Mitts,** remove pie plate to **Oven Pad.**

Approximately 220 calories and 0 grams of fat per serving

Sweetie Potato Pie

Sizzling Fried Rice

TAKE A QUICK TRIP TO THE ORIENT WITH THIS EASY, ONE-DISH SKILLET MEAL.
DON'T FORGET THE FORTUNE COOKIES!

MAKES 4 SERVINGS

Ingredients:

- I CUP WATER
- I GARLIC CLOVE
- I CUP INSTANT LONG GRAIN RICE, UNCOOKED
- I CUP FROZEN COMBINATION PEAS AND CARROTS
- 8 OUNCES DELI CHICKEN BREAST, CUT ½ INCH THICK
- 6 GREEN ONIONS WITH TOPS
- ½ CUP FRESH BEAN SPROUTS OR I CAN (8 OUNCES) SLICED WATER CHESTNUTS, DRAINED
- I TABLESPOON SOY SAUCE

Tools:

MEASURE-ALL® CUP
ADJUSTABLE SCOOP
ADJUSTABLE MEASURING SPOON
GENERATION II STIR-FRY SKILLET WITH 12" CLEAR VIEW LID
GARLIC PRESS
BAMBOO SPOON
13" X 9" CUTTING BOARD
GARNISHER OR CRINKLE CUTTER
QUIKUT PARING KNIFE

1 *Adult help:* Bring water to a boil in **Generation II Stir-Fry Skillet**. Press garlic into water using **Garlic Press**. Stir in rice and peas and carrots with **Bamboo Spoon**. Remove from heat and cover with lid. Let stand 5 minutes.

2 On **Cutting Board**, cut chicken into ½-inch cubes using **Garnisher** or **Crinkle Cutter** to equal 1½ cups. Cut root end off green onions and thinly slice with **Quikut Paring Knife** to make about ½ cup.

3 Stir chicken, green onions, bean sprouts and soy sauce into rice mixture.

4 *Adult help:* Return skillet to heat. Cook, uncovered, over medium heat 3-4 minutes or until thoroughly heated, stirring occasionally with Bamboo Spoon. Serve with additional soy sauce, if desired.

Approximately 190 calories and 2 grams of fat per serving

Shrimp Fried Rice:
Use 5 ounces frozen cooked large salad shrimp, thawed, instead of the chicken. Do not cut up.

Pork Fried Rice:
Use 8 ounces deli roast pork, cut ½ inch thick, instead of the chicken. Cut with **Garnisher** or **Crinkle Cutter** as recipe directs for chicken.

Cook's Tip:

MAKING THIS RECIPE IS A GREAT WAY TO USE UP LEFTOVER COOKED CHICKEN. WE'VE SUGGESTED USING COOKED CHICKEN FROM THE SUPERMARKET DELI COUNTER BECAUSE OF ITS CONVENIENCE. USING DELI MEATS IS A GOOD SHORTCUT IN RECIPES THAT CALL FOR COOKED MEAT.

Tool Tip:

FOR FRESH PRESSED GARLIC, SIMPLY PLACE THE GARLIC CLOVE, SKIN AND ALL, IN THE HOPPER OF THE **GARLIC PRESS** AND SQUEEZE HANDLES TOGETHER. THE GARLIC FLESH WILL BE FORCED THROUGH THE HOLES, WHILE THE SKIN STAYS IN THE PRESS.

Crinkle-Cut Potato Fingers

LEARN THE SECRETS TO MAKING YOUR
OWN SPECIALLY SEASONED HOME FRIES.

MAKES 6 SERVINGS

Ingredients:

4 MEDIUM BAKING POTATOES
   (1¾ POUNDS)

1 TABLESPOON MAYONNAISE

1 PACKAGE (0.4 OUNCES) DRY
   BUTTERMILK RECIPE RANCH
   SALAD DRESSING MIX

Tools:

ADJUSTABLE MEASURING SPOON

13" X 9" CUTTING BOARD

GARNISHER OR CRINKLE CUTTER

CLASSIC 2-QT. BATTER BOWL
   WITH LID

15" ROUND BAKING STONE WITH
   OVEN-TO-TABLE RACK

OVEN MITTS

1 Preheat oven to 400°F. Scrub potatoes clean and pat dry with paper towels, but do not peel.

2 *Adult help:* On **Cutting Board**, cut each potato in half lengthwise using **Garnisher** or **Crinkle Cutter**. Place potato halves, cut side down, on cutting board. Cut lengthwise into quarters.

3 Place potatoes in **Classic 2-Qt. Batter Bowl.** Add mayonnaise. Cover Batter Bowl with lid and shake until potatoes are evenly coated. Uncover and sprinkle dry salad dressing mix over coated potatoes. Cover with lid and shake again until potatoes are evenly coated.

4 Place **15" Round Baking Stone** in **Oven-To-Table Rack.** Arrange potatoes in a single layer on Baking Stone with the skin side of the potato touching the Baking Stone.

5 *Adult help:* Bake 35-40 minutes or until potatoes are golden brown. Using **Oven Mitts**, remove from oven.

Approximately 140 calories and 2 grams of fat per serving

Cook's Tip:

WITH THE SKINS LEFT ON, POTATOES KEEP MORE OF THEIR NUTRIENTS, THOSE THINGS THAT ARE GOOD FOR YOUR BODY. SOME PEOPLE THINK POTATOES WITH SKINS LEFT ON ARE MORE FLAVORFUL, BUT IF YOU KNOW YOU DON'T LIKE POTATO SKINS YOU CAN SCRUB THE POTATOES THEN PEEL THEM WITH THE **VEGETABLE PEELER** BEFORE CUTTING.

Tool Tip:

USING THE **GARNISHER OR CRINKLE CUTTER** IS A DECORATIVE WAY TO CUT POTATOES AND LOTS OF OTHER VEGETABLES. TO USE, PLACE ONE END OF **GARNISHER** OR **CRINKLE CUTTER** ON THE **CUTTING BOARD** AND USE A ROCKING MOTION TO CUT THROUGH FOODS. ALWAYS KEEP THE END OF THE **GARNISHER** OR **CRINKLE CUTTER** CLOSEST TO YOUR BODY FIRMLY ANCHORED TO THE **CUTTING BOARD** AND FINGERS OUT OF THE WAY.

Chicken Riddle Soup

Chicken Riddle Soup

WHY DID THE CHICKEN CROSS THE ROAD?
TO GET A CUP OF SOUP!

MAKES 6 SERVINGS

Ingredients:

- 1 SMALL ONION
- 2 MEDIUM CARROTS
- 2 CELERY STALKS
- 2 TABLESPOONS SNIPPED PARSLEY
- ¾ POUND BONELESS, SKINLESS CHICKEN BREAST HALVES (ABOUT 3 BREAST HALVES)
- ¼ TEASPOON SALT
- ⅛ TEASPOON GROUND BLACK PEPPER
- 1 GARLIC CLOVE
- 2 PACKAGES (2.8 OUNCES EACH) CHICKEN FLAVOR RAMEN NOODLE SOUP
- 5 CUPS WATER

Tools:

ADJUSTABLE MEASURING SPOONS
13" X 9" CUTTING BOARD
QUIKUT PARING KNIFE
FOOD CHOPPER
VEGETABLE PEELER
GARNISHER OR CRINKLE CUTTER
KITCHEN SHEARS
GENERATION II 4-QT. CASSEROLE
KITCHEN SPRITZER
GARLIC PRESS
BAMBOO SPOON
MEASURE-ALL® CUP

1 On **Cutting Board,** cut onion into small chunks using **Quikut Paring Knife** then chop using **Food Chopper.**

2 Peel carrots with **Vegetable Peeler.** Cut carrots and celery into ¼-inch-thick slices using **Garnisher** or **Crinkle Cutter.** Place parsley in a small, deep bowl. Snip with **Kitchen Shears** and set aside.

3 Rinse chicken under cold running water and pat dry with paper towels. Working over cutting board, use kitchen shears to cut chicken into small cubes.

4 Lightly spray **Generation II 4-Qt. Casserole** with vegetable oil using **Kitchen Spritzer.** Heat pan over medium-high heat 3 minutes. Add chicken cubes, onion, salt and pepper. Press garlic into pan using **Garlic Press.** Cook and stir with **Bamboo Spoon** 3-4 minutes or until chicken is no longer pink.

5 Stir in carrots, celery, seasoning packets from ramen noodles and water. Bring soup to a boil. Reduce heat to low and cover. Simmer 15 minutes.

6 Break noodles into small pieces and stir into simmering soup. Increase heat to medium and cook 3 minutes, stirring occasionally with Bamboo Spoon.

7 Just before serving, stir in parsley.

Approximately 190 calories and 9 grams of fat per serving (1¼ cups)

Cook's Tip:

WHEN WORKING WITH RAW CHICKEN IN A RECIPE, PLACE CHICKEN ON THE **CUTTING BOARD** ONLY AFTER ALL OTHER INGREDIENTS HAVE BEEN CHOPPED OR SLICED AND MOVED OFF OF THE CUTTING BOARD. BE SURE TO WASH YOUR HANDS, CUTTING BOARD AND **KITCHEN SHEARS** OR KNIVES WITH HOT, SOAPY WATER AFTER HANDLING RAW CHICKEN.

Corny Corn Muffins

YOU'LL LIKE THESE LITTLE GEMS MADE WITH
SWEET, GOLDEN NUGGETS OF CORN.

MAKES 2 DOZEN

Ingredients:

2 TABLESPOONS FINELY CHOPPED
   GREEN OR RED BELL PEPPER (OR
   A COMBINATION OF BOTH)
1 PACKAGE (7½-8½ OUNCES) CORN
   MUFFIN MIX (PLUS INGREDIENTS
   TO MAKE MUFFINS)
½ CUP THAWED FROZEN CORN OR
   CANNED CORN, DRAINED

Tools:

ADJUSTABLE SCOOP
ADJUSTABLE MEASURING SPOON
MEASURE-ALL® CUP
DELUXE MINI-MUFFIN PAN
QUIKUT PARING KNIFE
FOOD CHOPPER
13" X 9" CUTTING BOARD
CLASSIC 2-QT. BATTER BOWL
MIX 'N SCRAPER®
SMALL STAINLESS STEEL SCOOP
OVEN MITTS
OVEN PAD
NONSTICK COOLING RACK

1 Preheat oven to 350°F. Place paper liners in cups of **Deluxe Mini-Muffin Pan** or spray cups with nonstick cooking spray.

2 On **Cutting Board**, cut bell pepper into small chunks using **Quikut Paring Knife** then finely chop using **Food Chopper**.

3 In **Classic 2-Qt. Batter Bowl**, prepare corn muffin mix according to package directions mixing with **Mix 'N Scraper®**. Stir in bell pepper and corn.

4 Using small **Stainless Steel Scoop**, fill muffin cups ¾ full.

5 *Adult help:* Bake 12-13 minutes. (Do not overbake.) Using **Oven Mitts**, remove Mini-Muffin Pan to **Oven Pad**. Remove muffins from pan to **Nonstick Cooling Rack**. Serve warm.

Approximately 150 calories and 4 grams of fat per serving (3 muffins)

Cook's Tip:

WANT TO KNOW A GREAT COMBINATION? CORNY CORN MUFFINS WITH CHICKEN RIDDLE SOUP (PAGE 53) OR HOME ON THE RANGE CHILI (PAGE 43). DELICIOUS!

Tool Tip:

IF YOU'RE NOT USING PAPER LINERS, IT'S EASY TO LOOSEN AND REMOVE MUFFINS FROM CUPS WITH THE FLAT END OF THE CITRUS PEELER.

Speedy Stir-Fry Veggies

PICTURED ON PAGE 56

TAKE THESE VEGETABLES FOR A SPEEDY SPIN AROUND THE STIR-FRY SKILLET FOR FLAVORFUL, CRISP-TENDER VEGETABLES.

MAKES 6 SERVINGS (ABOUT 3 CUPS)

Ingredients:

6-8 FRESH WHOLE MUSHROOMS, WIPED CLEAN
1 MEDIUM RED BELL PEPPER
2 MEDIUM CARROTS
½ SMALL ONION
1 TABLESPOON OLIVE OIL
1½ CUPS FRESH BROCCOLI FLORETS
1 GARLIC CLOVE
½ TEASPOON DRIED OREGANO LEAVES
¼ TEASPOON SALT
DASH OF GROUND BLACK PEPPER

Tools:

QUIKUT PARING KNIFE
18" X 12" GROOVED CUTTING BOARD
EGG SLICER PLUS®
VEGETABLE PEELER
GARNISHER OR CRINKLE CUTTER
GARLIC PRESS
ADJUSTABLE SCOOP
ADJUSTABLE MEASURING SPOONS
GENERATION II STIR-FRY SKILLET
BAMBOO SPOON

1 On **Cutting Board**, cut thin slice off stem end of mushrooms using **Quikut Paring Knife**; discard ends. Using **Egg Slicer Plus®**, slice mushrooms to get about 1½ cups.

2 Cut bell pepper in half lengthwise and crosswise to get four pieces. Remove membranes and seeds. Cut bell pepper into thin short strips to get about 1 cup.

3 Peel carrots with **Vegetable Peeler**. Cut crosswise into ¼-inch-thick slices using **Garnisher** or **Crinkle Cutter** to get about ¾ cup. Cut onion into thin wedges.

4 *Adult help:* Heat oil in **Generation II Stir-Fry Skillet** over medium-high heat 3 minutes. Add broccoli, mushrooms, red bell pepper, carrot and onion. Press garlic into skillet using **Garlic Press**. Sprinkle oregano, salt and black pepper over vegetables. Stir and toss vegetables with **Bamboo Spoon** 3-4 minutes or until vegetables are tender but still crisp.

Approximately 40 calories and 2 grams of fat per serving

Cook's Tips:

FRESH BROCCOLI FLORETS (THE TOPS OF THE BROCCOLI) COME IN CONVENIENT PACKAGES AND CAN BE FOUND IN THE FRESH PRODUCE SECTION OF THE SUPERMARKET.

BECAUSE STIR-FRYING IS SUCH A QUICK METHOD OF COOKING IT'S IMPORTANT TO HAVE ALL OF YOUR INGREDIENTS ASSEMBLED, CUT, MEASURED AND READY TO GO. IN THIS VEGETABLE STIR-FRY RECIPE, MANY OTHER VEGETABLES WOULD BE EQUALLY AS GOOD TASTING. YOU CAN USE CAULIFLOWER FLORETS, CELERY SLICES, ZUCCHINI SLICES, GREEN BELL PEPPER STRIPS OR PEA PODS INSTEAD OF ANY OF THE ABOVE VEGETABLES. JUST KEEP THE MEASURED AMOUNTS THE SAME.

Tool Tip:

THE **GENERATION II STIR-FRY SKILLET** IS DEEP WITH HIGH SIDES TO ALLOW MORE SPACE TO STIR AND TOSS THE VEGETABLES FOR FAST, EVEN COOKING.

Crispy Chip Chicken, Speedy Stir-Fry Veggies p. 55

Crispy Chip Chicken

EVERYBODY WANTS TO KNOW THE SECRET TO YOUR CRISPY OVEN-BAKED CHICKEN.
DO YOU DARE TELL THEM?

MAKES 6 SERVINGS

Ingredients:

4½ CUPS CHILI CHEESE OR
   BARBECUE FLAVOR CORN CHIPS
  1 EGG
  1 TABLESPOON MILK
  1 BROILER-FRYER CHICKEN, CUT
    UP (3-3½ POUNDS)
  2 TABLESPOONS BUTTER OR
    MARGARINE

Tools:

ADJUSTABLE SCOOP
ADJUSTABLE MEASURING SPOON
MY SAFE CUTTER™
13" X 9" CUTTING BOARD
DOUGH AND PIZZA ROLLER
STONEWARE 9" PIE PLATE
CLASSIC 2-QT. BATTER BOWL
10" WHISK
KITCHEN SHEARS
9" X 13" BAKER
COVERED MICRO-COOKER®
OVEN MITTS
STONEWARE TRIVET

1 Preheat oven to 375°F. Place chips in large resealable plastic bag. Using **Dough and Pizza Roller**, crush chips to make 2 cups coarse crumbs. Pour into **Stoneware 9" Pie Plate** and set aside.

2 In **Classic 2-Qt. Batter Bowl**, mix egg and milk using **10" Whisk**.

3 Rinse chicken pieces under cold running water and pat dry with paper towels. Trim off any extra skin or fat using **Kitchen Shears**. Dip chicken in egg mixture, one piece at a time, then roll in crumbs to coat evenly. (Press crumbs against the chicken so they will stick.) Place chicken, meaty side up, in **9" x 13" Baker**. Sprinkle chicken with any remaining crumbs. (Discard egg mixture.)

4 Place butter in **Covered Micro-Cooker®**. Microwave on HIGH 30 seconds or until melted. Slowly pour butter over chicken.

5 *Adult help:* Bake 1 hour or until chicken is no longer pink in center. Using **Oven Mitts**, remove Baker to **Stoneware Trivet**.

Approximately 450 calories and 30 grams of fat per serving

Cook's Tips:

YOU CAN USE REGULAR FLAVOR CORN CHIPS INSTEAD OF THE CHILI CHEESE CORN CHIPS. JUST ADD 2 TEASPOONS CHILI POWDER TO THE CRUMBS.

IT'S IMPORTANT TO PRACTICE FOOD SAFETY RULES WHEN COOKING WITH CHICKEN. ALWAYS WASH YOUR HANDS, **CUTTING BOARD,** TOOLS AND WORK SURFACE WITH HOT, SOAPY WATER IMMEDIATELY AFTER HANDLING RAW CHICKEN TO PREVENT SPREADING BACTERIA TO OTHER FOODS.

Tempting Tuna Melt

IMPRESS YOUR FAMILY WITH THIS WARM, TASTY SANDWICH RING.
IT'S GUARANTEED TO MAKE A SPLASH!

MAKES 8 SERVINGS

Ingredients:

⅔ CUP MAYONNAISE

¼ CUP SWEET PICKLE RELISH

2 CANS (6 OUNCES EACH) WATER-PACKED TUNA, DRAINED

¼ CUP CHOPPED CELERY

2 TABLESPOONS FINELY CHOPPED ONION

I CUP (4 OUNCES) SHREDDED CHEDDAR CHEESE

2 PACKAGES (8 OUNCES EACH) REFRIGERATED CRESCENT ROLLS

I MEDIUM RED OR GREEN BELL PEPPER

I CUP SHREDDED LETTUCE

Tools:

MEASURE-ALL® CUP

ADJUSTABLE SCOOP

ADJUSTABLE MEASURING SPOON

I-QT. BATTER BOWL

CLASSIC 2-QT. BATTER BOWL

MY SAFE CUTTER™

FOOD CHOPPER

18" X 12" GROOVED CUTTING BOARD

BAMBOO SPOON

13" ROUND BAKING STONE WITH OVEN-TO-TABLE RACK

MEDIUM STAINLESS STEEL SCOOP

OVEN MITTS

V-SHAPED CUTTER

GARNISHER OR CRINKLE CUTTER

SLICE 'N SERVE®

1 Preheat oven to 375°F. In **1-Qt. Batter Bowl**, mix mayonnaise and pickle relish using **Bamboo Spoon.**

2 Place drained tuna in **Classic 2-Qt. Batter Bowl.** Flake (break apart) tuna with spoon.

3 On **Cutting Board,** cut celery and onion into small chunks using **My Safe Cutter™.** Chop celery using **Food Chopper.** Finely chop the onion. Add celery, onion, cheese and ¼ cup of the mayonnaise mixture to the tuna. Mix well. Refrigerate remaining mayonnaise mixture.

4 Unroll crescent dough and separate into 16 triangles. On **13" Round Baking Stone,** arrange triangles in a circle with the wide ends of the triangles overlapping in the center and points toward the outside. (There should be a 5-inch diameter open circle in the center of the Baking Stone. The tips of the rolls will hang off the edge of the Stone for now.)

5 Using medium **Stainless Steel Scoop,** scoop tuna mixture onto the wide ends of the overlapping triangles. Bring the outside points of the triangles up over the filling and tuck under wide ends of dough at center of ring. (Filling will not be completely covered). Place Baking Stone in **Oven-To-Table Rack.**

6 *Adult help:* Bake 20-25 minutes or until deep golden brown. Using **Oven Mitts,** remove from oven.

7 Using **V-Shaped Cutter,** cut around top of bell pepper. Separate the two pieces and remove the membrane and seeds. Fill with the remaining mayonnaise mixture and place in center of ring. Using **Garnisher** or **Crinkle Cutter,** cut lettuce into thin strands. Arrange lettuce around pepper. To serve, cut with **Slice 'N Serve®.**

Approximately 460 calories and 32 grams of fat per serving

Tempting Tuna Melt

Rainy Day Cookie Art p. 62

Sweet Treats

The ultimate chapter of gooey treats, giant cookies and cool desserts.

Rainy Day Cookie Art

LET YOUR ARTISTIC TALENTS SHINE WHEN YOU PAINT AN
EDIBLE MASTERPIECE ON A COOKIE DOUGH CANVAS.

MAKES 16 SERVINGS

Ingredients:

- 1 PACKAGE (18 OUNCES) REFRIGERATED SUGAR COOKIE DOUGH
- ALL-PURPOSE FLOUR
- 2 EGGS (YOLKS SEPARATED FROM WHITES)
- ½ TEASPOON WATER
- ASSORTED LIQUID OR PASTE FOOD COLORS
- SMALL CANDIES OR MINIATURE SEMI-SWEET CHOCOLATE MORSELS (IF DESIRED)

Tools:

KITCHEN SHEARS

ADJUSTABLE MEASURING SPOON

12" X 15" RECTANGLE BAKING STONE WITH OVEN-TO-TABLE RACK

DOUGH AND PIZZA ROLLER

BREAD TUBES

THE CORER™

QUIKUT PARING KNIFE

EGG SEPARATOR

1-QT. BATTER BOWL

10" WHISK

OVEN MITTS

NONSTICK COOLING RACK

SERRATED BREAD KNIFE

MINI-SERVING SPATULA

1 Preheat oven to 350°F. Remove cookie dough from wrapper by cutting off wrapper ends and down seam with **Kitchen Shears**. Place roll of dough crosswise in middle of **12" x 15" Rectangle Baking Stone**; let stand about 5 minutes to soften. Sprinkle **Dough and Pizza Roller** with flour and roll dough into 1 large rectangle, 11 x 14 inches big and about ¼ inch thick.

2 Dip one end of **Bread Tubes** and **The Corer™** in flour. Press designs into dough for a "sunny flower garden" or a "creepy crawling bugs" picture. Add details using **Quikut Paring Knife.**

3 See Cook's Tip on separating egg yolks from whites. In **1-Qt. Batter Bowl,** mix egg yolks and water with **10" Whisk.**

4 Carefully divide egg yolk mixture into several small bowls or custard cups. For each desired color, add 1-3 drops food color to each cup and mix well.

5 Paint cookie dough using small craft paint brushes. If "paint" thickens, stir in a few drops of water. Decorate cookie with small candies, if desired. Place Baking Stone in **Oven-To-Table Rack.**

6 *Adult help:* Bake 17-18 minutes or until light golden brown. Using **Oven Mitts,** remove Baking Stone to **Nonstick Cooling Rack.** Cool 10 minutes. Carefully run **Serrated Bread Knife** under cookie to loosen from Baking Stone; cool completely.

7 Cut cookie into pieces; serve with **Mini-Serving Spatula.**

Approximately 140 calories and 6 grams of fat per serving

Cook's Tip:

TO SEPARATE AN EGG, PLACE **EGG SEPARATOR** OVER RIM OF A SMALL BOWL. CRACK EGG SHELL ON EDGE OF BOWL. SEPARATE THE SHELL SO THE EGG DROPS INTO THE WIRE BASKET, ALLOWING THE EGG WHITE TO FALL INTO THE BOWL. LEFTOVER EGG WHITES CAN BE ADDED TO WHOLE EGGS TO MAKE SCRAMBLED EGGS OR OMELETS.

Spiced Carrot Snack Cake

JUST ADD CARROTS AND APPLESAUCE TO A PACKAGED
QUICK BREAD MIX FOR A SUPER SIMPLE SPICY CAKE.

MAKES 9 SERVINGS

Ingredients:

- 1 PACKAGE (17.4 OUNCES)
  CINNAMON SWIRL
  QUICK BREAD MIX
- 2 LARGE CARROTS, SHREDDED
  (1 CUP)
- ½ CUP NATURAL APPLESAUCE
- 2 EGGS
- 3 TABLESPOONS VEGETABLE OIL

Tools:

MEASURE-ALL® CUP

ADJUSTABLE MEASURING SPOON

9" SQUARE BAKER

KITCHEN SPRITZER

CLASSIC 2-QT. BATTER BOWL

VEGETABLE PEELER

13" X 9" CUTTING BOARD

QUIKUT PARING KNIFE

DELUXE CHEESE GRATER

MIX 'N SCRAPER®

CAKE TESTER

OVEN MITTS

NONSTICK COOLING RACK

MINI-SERVING SPATULA

1 Preheat oven to 350°F. Lightly spray bottom of **9" Square Baker** with vegetable oil using **Kitchen Spritzer**.

2 In **Classic 2-Qt. Batter Bowl**, combine half of the cinnamon mixture from packet (½ cup) and quick bread mix. Set remaining cinnamon mixture aside.

3 Peel carrots with **Vegetable Peeler**. On **Cutting Board**, trim ends from carrots then cut carrots into 2-inch pieces with **Quikut Paring Knife**. Using **Deluxe Cheese Grater** fitted with coarse shredding drum, shred carrots, a few pieces at a time, to make 1 cup. Add carrots to Batter Bowl.

4 Add applesauce, eggs and oil to Batter Bowl. Stir with **Mix 'N Scraper®** until well blended, about 50-75 strokes. Spread batter evenly in Baker. Sprinkle with remaining cinnamon mixture.

5 *Adult help:* Bake 25-30 minutes or until **Cake Tester** inserted in center comes out clean. Using **Oven Mitts**, remove Baker to **Nonstick Cooling Rack**. Cool completely. Cut into squares and serve using **Mini-Serving Spatula**.

Approximately 220 calories and 9 grams of fat per serving

Cook's Tip:

FOR EXTRA FLAVOR AND CRUNCH, ADD CHOPPED NUTS TO THIS SNACK CAKE. CHOP ½ CUP WALNUTS OR PECANS ON CUTTING BOARD USING FOOD CHOPPER. ADD ALONG WITH THE CARROTS TO BATTER BOWL.

Shortcut Strawberry Shortcakes

Shortcut Strawberry Shortcakes

WE'VE GOT THE SHORTEST ROUTE TO MAKING
ONE TOTALLY TERRIFIC DESSERT!

MAKES 8 SERVINGS

Ingredients:

SHORTCAKES

- 1 PACKAGE (17.3 OUNCES) GRAND-SIZE REFRIGERATED BUTTERMILK BISCUITS
- 2 TABLESPOONS SUGAR
- ¼ TEASPOON GROUND CINNAMON

FRUIT TOPPING

- 2 PINTS FRESH STRAWBERRIES
- 3 KIWI FRUIT
- 1-2 TABLESPOONS SUGAR
- 1½ CUPS THAWED FROZEN WHIPPED TOPPING

Tools:

ADJUSTABLE SCOOP

ADJUSTABLE MEASURING SPOONS

15" ROUND BAKING STONE WITH OVEN-TO-TABLE RACK

FLOUR/SUGAR SHAKER

OVEN MITTS

OVEN PAD

MINI-SERVING SPATULA

NONSTICK COOLING RACK

TOMATO CORER

EGG SLICER PLUS®

CLASSIC 2-QT. BATTER BOWL

VEGETABLE PEELER

MY SAFE CUTTER™

SUPER SCRAPER

13" X 9" CUTTING BOARD

EASY ACCENT® DECORATOR

1 Preheat oven to 375°F. For shortcakes, place biscuits 1-2 inches apart on **15" Round Baking Stone.** Combine sugar and cinnamon in **Flour/Sugar Shaker.** Sprinkle some of the cinnamon mixture evenly over tops of biscuits. Turn biscuits over and sprinkle with remaining mixture. Place Baking Stone in **Oven-To-Table Rack.**

2 *Adult help:* Bake 11-15 minutes or until golden brown. Using **Oven Mitts,** remove Baking Stone to **Oven Pad.** Using **Mini-Serving Spatula,** remove shortcakes to **Nonstick Cooling Rack.** Cool 10 minutes.

3 Meanwhile, prepare fruit topping. Gently wash strawberries with cool water. Choose 8 "pretty" strawberries to use for decoration and set aside. Using **Tomato Corer,** remove stems from remaining strawberries. Using **Egg Slicer Plus®,** slice strawberries into **Classic 2-Qt. Batter Bowl.** Peel kiwis with **Vegetable Peeler** and slice using Egg Slicer Plus®. Using **My Safe Cutter™,** cut kiwi slices in half on **Cutting Board** and add to strawberries.

4 Add sugar to fruit mixture and mix gently using **Super Scraper.** Split each shortcake in half crosswise using My Safe Cutter™.

5 To serve, place bottom halves of shortcakes on individual small plates. Top each with some of the fruit mixture and cover with top half of shortcake. Attach **Decorating Tip** to **Easy Accent® Decorator** and fill tube with whipped topping. Top each shortcake with whipped topping and a whole strawberry for decoration.

Approximately 290 calories and 13 grams of fat per serving

Ooey Gooey Caramel Chocolate Dunk

JUST ABOUT ANYTHING TASTES GREAT SMOTHERED IN THIS WARM CARAMEL AND CHOCOLATE DIP.
WE'VE GIVEN YOU JUST A FEW IDEAS.

MAKES 16 SERVINGS (2 CUPS DIP)

Ingredients:

- 1 PACKAGE (14 OUNCES) CARAMELS (ABOUT 50)
- 1 CAN (5 OUNCES) EVAPORATED MILK
- ½ CUP SEMI-SWEET CHOCOLATE MORSELS
- ½ TEASPOON VANILLA
- DIPPERS (YOU CHOOSE!): FRESH STRAWBERRIES, APPLE OR PEAR WEDGES, PRETZELS, COOKIES OR ANGEL FOOD OR POUND CAKE CUBES

Tools:

ADJUSTABLE SCOOP
ADJUSTABLE MEASURING SPOON
CAN OPENER
MINI-BAKING BOWL
BAMBOO SPOON
OVEN MITTS
OVEN PAD
APPLE WEDGER
13" X 9" CUTTING BOARD

1 Preheat oven to 350°F. Unwrap caramels and place in **Mini-Baking Bowl**. Add evaporated milk, chocolate morsels and vanilla and stir with **Bamboo Spoon**.

2 *Adult help:* Bake 30 minutes. Using **Oven Mitts**, remove Mini-Baking Bowl to **Oven Pad**. Stir with Bamboo Spoon until the mixture is smooth. (Don't worry if there are a few small pieces of unmelted caramel.)

3 Serve with your favorite dippers.

Approximately 140 calories and 4 grams of fat per serving (2 tablespoons of dip)

Cook's Tip:

TO PREPARE THIS DIP IN THE MICROWAVE OVEN, PLACE DIP INGREDIENTS IN **MINI-BAKING BOWL** AS DIRECTED IN STEP #1. PLACE IN MICROWAVE OVEN AND MICROWAVE ON **HIGH** 3 MINUTES. *ADULT HELP:* USING **OVEN MITTS**, REMOVE MINI-BAKING BOWL TO **OVEN PAD** AND STIR WITH **BAMBOO SPOON**. RETURN TO MICROWAVE OVEN AND CONTINUE MICROWAVING **30** SECONDS TO 1 MINUTE OR UNTIL CARAMEL IS MELTED. STIR UNTIL SMOOTH.

Tool Tip:

WHEN MAKING APPLE OR PEAR WEDGES, STAND FRUIT UPRIGHT ON A CUTTING BOARD, CENTER **APPLE WEDGER** OVER STEM OF FRUIT AND PRESS STRAIGHT DOWN TO CORE AND SLICE FRUIT. FOR THINNER SLICES, CUT WEDGES IN HALF LENGTHWISE WITH **QUIKUT PARING KNIFE**.

Ooey Gooey Caramel Chocolate Dunk

Slammin' Jammin' Berry Bars

PICTURED ON PAGE 70

THESE BARS ARE SO AWESOMELY GOOD, YOU'LL BE TEMPTED
TO HAVE ANOTHER...BUT WHO'S KEEPING SCORE?

MAKES 16 BARS

Ingredients:

1½ CUPS ALL-PURPOSE FLOUR

1¼ CUPS QUICK OR OLD-FASHIONED OATS

½ CUP PACKED BROWN SUGAR

¾ CUP (1½ STICKS) BUTTER OR MARGARINE

½ CUP STRAWBERRY OR RASPBERRY PRESERVES

1 CUP FRESH OR FROZEN BLUEBERRIES

Tools:

ADJUSTABLE SCOOP

QUIKUT PARING KNIFE

X 9" CUTTING BOARD

CLASSIC 2-QT. BATTER BOWL

PASTRY BLENDER

9" SQUARE BAKER

ALL-PURPOSE SPREADER

OVEN MITTS

NONSTICK COOLING RACK

MINI-SERVING SPATULA

1 Preheat oven to 375°F. In **Classic 2-Qt. Batter Bowl**, mix flour, oats and brown sugar with **Pastry Blender.**

2 On **Cutting Board**, cut butter into small pieces using **Quikut Paring Knife** and add to flour mixture. Using Pastry Blender, cut in butter until the mixture is crumbly. Measure out 1 cup of the crumb mixture and set it aside for the topping. Press the remaining crumb mixture onto bottom of **9" Square Baker.**

3 Spread preserves over crust using **All-Purpose Spreader.** Sprinkle evenly with blueberries. Sprinkle reserved crumb mixture evenly over blueberries.

4 *Adult help:* Bake 35-40 minutes or until golden brown. Using **Oven Mitts**, remove Baker to **Nonstick Cooling Rack.**

5 Cool completely. Cut into squares and remove from Baker using **Mini-Serving Spatula.**

Approximately 180 calories and 9 grams of fat per serving (1 bar)

Tool Tip:

USE THE ALL PURPOSE SPREADER TO MAKE THAT LUNCH BOX FAVORITE — PB&J SANDWICHES.

Thumbs Up Thumbprints

PICTURED ON PAGE 70

CHOCOLATE AND NUTS STAR IN THIS
WINNING COOKIE COMBINATION.

MAKES 1½ DOZEN COOKIES

Ingredients:

- I CUP ALL-PURPOSE FLOUR
- ⅓ CUP SUGAR
- ½ CUP (I STICK) BUTTER OR MARGARINE
- I EGG (YOLK SEPARATED FROM WHITE)
- I TEASPOON VANILLA
- ½ CUP HONEY ROASTED PEANUTS, CASHEWS OR PECANS
- 18 FOIL-WRAPPED MILK CHOCOLATE OR WHITE AND CHOCOLATE STRIPED CANDIES, UNWRAPPED

Tools:

- ADJUSTABLE SCOOP
- ADJUSTABLE MEASURING SPOON
- 13" X 9" CUTTING BOARD
- QUIKUT PARING KNIFE
- EGG SEPARATOR
- I-QT. BATTER BOWL
- IO" WHISK
- FOOD CHOPPER
- SMALL STAINLESS STEEL SCOOP
- 15" ROUND BAKING STONE WITH OVEN-TO-TABLE RACK
- OVEN MITTS
- OVEN PAD
- NONSTICK COOLING RACK
- MINI-SERVING SPATULA

1 Preheat oven to 350°F. Place flour and sugar in resealable, gallon-size plastic bag. Seal bag and shake to mix.

2 On **Cutting Board,** cut butter into small pieces using **Quikut Paring Knife;** add to bag. Press air out of bag and seal. Mix butter into flour mixture by squeezing bag with your fingers until thoroughly combined.

3 To separate egg yolk from white, place **Egg Separator** over rim of **1-Qt. Batter Bowl.** Crack egg shell on edge of Bowl; separate shell so egg drops into wire basket, allowing egg white to fall into Bowl. Drop yolk into bag along with vanilla; press air out and seal. Squeeze mixture in bag until thoroughly combined.

4 Lightly beat egg white with **10" Whisk.** Using **Food Chopper,** finely chop nuts.

5 For each cookie, use small **Stainless Steel Scoop** to measure a level scoopful of dough into your hand and roll into a ball. Dip each ball into beaten egg white then roll in nuts. Place balls 2 inches apart on **15" Round Baking Stone.** Press your thumb deeply into the center of each ball. Throw away any leftover egg white or nuts. Place Baking Stone in **Oven-To-Table Rack.**

6 *Adult help:* Bake 16 minutes. Using **Oven Mitts,** remove Baking Stone to **Oven Pad.**

7 Lightly press a chocolate candy in the center of each cookie. Let stand on Baking Stone 3 minutes. Remove cookies to **Nonstick Cooling Rack** with **Mini-Serving Spatula.** Cool completely.

Approximately 110 calories and 7 grams of fat per serving (1 cookie)

Cook's Tip:

YOU CAN USE RED OR GREEN MARASCHINO CHERRIES INSTEAD OF THE CHOCOLATE CANDIES, IF YOU LIKE.

Mini Brownie Buttons, Slammin' Jammin' Berry Bars p. 68, Thumbs Up Thumbprints p. 69

Mini Brownie Buttons

THESE FUDGY BROWNIE BITES ARE SUCH GOOD LUNCH BOX TREATS
THAT YOU WON'T WANT TO TRADE THEM AWAY!

MAKES 12 SERVINGS (24 BROWNIES)

Ingredients:

⅓ CUP STICK BUTTER OR
MARGARINE

2 SQUARES (1 OUNCE EACH)
UNSWEETENED BAKING
CHOCOLATE

¾ CUP SUGAR

2 EGGS

½ TEASPOON VANILLA

¾ CUP ALL-PURPOSE FLOUR

½ CUP MINIATURE CANDY-COATED
CHOCOLATE PIECES

Tools:

MY SAFE CUTTER™

13" X 9" CUTTING BOARD

ADJUSTABLE SCOOP

ADJUSTABLE MEASURING SPOON

DELUXE MINI-MUFFIN PAN

GENERATION II 2-QT. SAUCEPAN

BAMBOO SPOON

OVEN PAD

SMALL STAINLESS STEEL SCOOP

OVEN MITTS

NONSTICK COOLING RACK

1 Heat oven to 325°F. Place paper liners in cups of **Deluxe Mini-Muffin Pan** or spray cups with nonstick cooking spray; set aside.

2 In **Generation II 2-Qt. Saucepan,** melt butter and chocolate over very low heat, stirring constantly with **Bamboo Spoon.** Remove saucepan from heat to **Oven Pad** and let cool 5 minutes.

3 Stir in sugar, eggs and vanilla. Add flour and ¼ cup of the candies and mix well.

4 Using small **Stainless Steel Scoop,** fill muffin cups with 1 scoop batter. Sprinkle remaining candies over batter.

5 *Adult help:* Bake 12-13 minutes. (Do not overbake.) Using **Oven Mitts,** remove pan to **Nonstick Cooling Rack.** Cool 5 minutes and remove brownies from pan. Cool. Store in airtight container at room temperature.

Approximately 200 calories and 11 grams of fat per serving (2 brownies)

Cook's Tip:

FOR BEST RESULTS WHEN BAKING, USE BUTTER OR MARGARINE PACKAGED IN STICKS. IN THE GROCERY STORE, CHECK LABELS CAREFULLY. VEGETABLE OIL SPREADS MAY LOOK THE SAME BUT REALLY DON'T WORK AS WELL IN MOST COOKIES, CAKES AND DESSERTS. STICKS OF BUTTER AND MARGARINE COME WITH THE MEASUREMENTS MARKED ON THE WRAPPER SO YOU'LL BE SURE TO GET THE EXACT AMOUNT YOU NEED.

Tool Tip:

USE THE FLAT END OF THE **CITRUS PEELER** TO REMOVE BROWNIES FROM MUFFIN CUPS.

The Best Banana Cream Pie

HERE'S A PIE THAT'S TONS BETTER TASTING THAN
STORE-BOUGHT, AND YOU MADE IT YOURSELF!

MAKES 8 SERVINGS

Ingredients:

CRUST
½ PACKAGE (15 OUNCES)
  REFRIGERATED PIE CRUSTS
  (I CRUST)
2 TEASPOONS SUGAR
¼ TEASPOON GROUND CINNAMON

FILLING
2 LARGE BANANAS
1½ CUPS MILK
I PACKAGE (3.4 OUNCES) BANANA
  CREAM OR VANILLA INSTANT
  PUDDING AND PIE FILLING
I CONTAINER (12 OUNCES) FROZEN
  WHIPPED TOPPING, THAWED

Tools:

MEASURE-ALL® CUP
ADJUSTABLE MEASURING SPOON
FLOUR/SUGAR SHAKER
KITCHEN SPRITZER
STONEWARE 9" PIE PLATE
OVEN MITTS
NONSTICK COOLING RACK
MY SAFE CUTTER™
I3" X 9" CUTTING BOARD
EGG SLICER PLUS®
CLASSIC 2-QT. BATTER BOWL
IO" WHISK
SUPER SCRAPER
EASY ACCENT® DECORATOR

1 Preheat oven to 450°F. For crust, let crust stand in pouch at room temperature 15 minutes. Combine sugar and cinnamon in **Flour/Sugar Shaker.**

2 Remove crust from pouch and unfold. Remove plastic sheets and press out folds. Lightly spray with water using **Kitchen Spritzer.** Sprinkle with sugar-cinnamon mixture.

3 Place crust in **Stoneware 9" Pie Plate.** Using your fingertips, press the crust firmly against the bottom and side of the pie plate. (Be careful not to stretch the crust.) Fold the extra crust under to form a thick, flat edge even with the rim of the pie plate. Press around the edge with a fork. Prick the bottom and side of crust with fork about 20 times.

4 *Adult help:* Bake 9-10 minutes or until lightly browned. Using **Oven Mitts,** remove pie plate to **Nonstick Cooling Rack.** Cool 30 minutes.

5 For filling, peel bananas and cut into 2-inch pieces using **My Safe Cutter™.** Slice bananas with **Egg Slicer Plus®** and arrange in bottom of pie crust.

6 Pour milk into **Classic 2-Qt. Batter Bowl.** Add pudding mix and beat with **10" Whisk** 2 minutes or until pudding begins to thicken. Gently mix in 1 cup of the whipped topping using **Super Scraper.** Quickly spread pudding mixture over bananas. Refrigerate 1 hour.

7 Attach **Closed Star Tip** to **Easy Accent® Decorator** and fill tube with remaining whipped topping. Hold decorator straight up and down with tip about 1 inch above top of pie. Gently squeeze down trigger to form a star. Stop pressure and pull decorator up. Continue to make stars very close together until entire top of pie is covered with whipped topping. Refill decorator as needed.

8 Cut into wedges and serve immediately or refrigerate.

The Best Banana Cream Pie

Pineapple Crown Cake

AN UPSIDE-DOWN DESSERT FIT FOR ANY KING OR QUEEN.

MAKES 8 SERVINGS

Ingredients:

¼ CUP MARASCHINO CHERRIES

1 CAN (8 OUNCES) CRUSHED PINEAPPLE

2 TABLESPOONS BUTTER OR MARGARINE

¼ CUP PACKED BROWN SUGAR

1 PACKAGE (9 OUNCES) YELLOW CAKE MIX (PLUS INGREDIENTS TO MAKE CAKE)

THAWED FROZEN WHIPPED TOPPING (IF DESIRED)

Tools:

ADJUSTABLE SCOOP

QUIKUT PARING KNIFE

13" X 9" CUTTING BOARD

MEASURE-ALL® CUP

FOOD CHOPPER

CAN OPENER

COVERED MICRO-COOKER®

SKINNY SCRAPER

8" MINI-BAKER

CLASSIC 2-QT. BATTER BOWL

10" WHISK

SUPER SCRAPER

CAKE TESTER

OVEN MITTS

NONSTICK COOLING RACK

1 Preheat oven to 350°F. Place maraschino cherries on a paper towel to drain off juice. On **Cutting Board**, chop cherries using **Food Chopper** and set aside. Place pineapple in colander to drain.

2 Place butter in **Covered Micro-Cooker®**. Microwave on HIGH 30 seconds or until melted. Using **Skinny Scraper**, mix melted butter and brown sugar in **8" Mini-Baker** until well blended. Spread evenly to cover bottom of Mini-Baker.

3 Spread pineapple over brown sugar mixture and sprinkle with cherries. Set aside.

4 Prepare cake mix according to package directions in **Classic 2-Qt. Batter Bowl** using **10" Whisk.**

5 Pour cake batter over fruit mixture in Mini-Baker using **Super Scraper** to remove batter from Bowl.

6 *Adult help:* Bake 40-45 minutes or until **Cake Tester** inserted in center comes out clean. Using **Oven Mitts**, remove Mini-Baker to **Nonstick Cooling Rack** and cool 5 minutes. Loosen edge of cake from Mini-Baker using **Quikut Paring Knife**. Place serving plate upside down over top of cake and carefully turn over. Carefully remove Mini-Baker. Serve warm or at room temperature with whipped topping, if desired.

Approximately 210 calories and 7 grams of fat per serving

Cook's Tip:

IT'S FINE TO USE THE JUICE FROM THE CRUSHED PINEAPPLE IN YOUR CAKE. JUST DRAIN PINEAPPLE IN A COLANDER THAT'S SET OVER A BOWL TO CATCH THE JUICE. POUR JUICE INTO **MEASURE-ALL® CUP** AND ADD ENOUGH WATER TO MAKE ½ CUP LIQUID. USE THIS LIQUID IN PLACE OF THE WATER TO PREPARE CAKE BATTER.

Pineapple Crown Cake

Striped Pudding Parfaits

Striped Pudding Parfaits

IF YOU LIKE CONSTRUCTION PROJECTS, YOU'LL LOVE "BUILDING"
THESE TOWERING FRUIT AND PUDDING CREATIONS.

MAKES 6 SERVINGS

Ingredients:

2 CUPS COLD MILK

1 PACKAGE (3.9 OUNCES)
CHOCOLATE INSTANT PUDDING
AND PIE FILLING

2 CUPS THAWED FROZEN WHIPPED
TOPPING

1 PINT STRAWBERRIES

2 MEDIUM BANANAS

½ CUP HONEY GRANOLA CRUNCH
(PAGE 23)

Tools:

MEASURE-ALL® CUP

CLASSIC 2-QT. BATTER BOWL

10" WHISK

EASY ACCENT® DECORATOR

MEDIUM STAINLESS STEEL SCOOP

TOMATO CORER

MY SAFE CUTTER™

13" X 9" CUTTING BOARD

EGG SLICER PLUS®

1 Pour milk into **Classic 2-Qt. Batter Bowl.** Add pudding mix and beat with **10" Whisk** for 2 minutes until pudding begins to thicken. Refrigerate 5 minutes.

2 Attach **Open Star Tip** to **Easy Accent® Decorator.** Using medium **Stainless Steel Scoop,** fill tube with whipped topping.

3 Remove stems from strawberries using **Tomato Corer.** Peel bananas. On **Cutting Board,** cut bananas into 2-inch pieces using **My Safe Cutter™.** Slice strawberries and bananas using **Egg Slicer Plus®.**

4 In 6 (6-8 ounce) parfait or clear plastic drinking glasses, layer pudding, whipped topping, strawberries, bananas and granola any way you like. Top with a strawberry fan or extra banana slices, if desired.

Approximately 260 calories and 8 grams of fat per serving

Cook's Tip:

BY USING OTHER FLAVORS OF PUDDING AND DIFFERENT FRUITS YOU CAN CREATE AN ALMOST ENDLESS NUMBER OF FLAVOR COMBINATIONS. JUST LET YOUR IMAGINATION RUN WILD!

Tool Tip:

THE MEDIUM **STAINLESS STEEL SCOOP** IS THE PERFECT TOOL FOR SCOOPING PUDDING INTO THE PARFAIT GLASSES.

Giant Pizza Cookie

LET YOUR IMAGINATION GO WILD AND TOP THIS CHOCOLATEY
GOOD COOKIE WITH SOME OF YOUR CANDY JAR FAVORITES!

MAKES 12 SERVINGS

Ingredients:

- 1 CUP ALL-PURPOSE FLOUR
- ¾ CUP QUICK OR OLD-FASHIONED OATS
- ½ TEASPOON BAKING SODA
- ¼ TEASPOON SALT
- ½ CUP (1 STICK) BUTTER OR MAR-GARINE, ROOM TEMPERATURE
- ½ CUP PACKED BROWN SUGAR
- 1 EGG
- ½ TEASPOON VANILLA
- 1 CUP SEMI-SWEET CHOCOLATE MORSELS
- 1 CUP PREPARED MILK CHOCOLATE FROSTING
- RED FRUIT SNACK ROLLS, GUMDROPS, CANDY-COATED CHOCOLATE PIECES AND WHITE CHOCOLATE

Tools:

ADJUSTABLE SCOOP
ADJUSTABLE MEASURING SPOON
1-QT. BATTER BOWL
BAMBOO SPOON
CLASSIC 2-QT. BATTER BOWL
13" ROUND BAKING STONE WITH OVEN-TO-TABLE RACK
OVEN MITTS
NONSTICK COOLING RACK
SKINNY SCRAPER
THE CORER™
KITCHEN SHEARS
DELUXE CHEESE GRATER
PIZZA CUTTER

1 Preheat oven to 350°F. In **1-Qt. Batter Bowl**, mix flour, oats, baking soda and salt with **Bamboo Spoon** and set aside.

2 In **Classic 2-Qt. Batter Bowl**, beat butter and brown sugar until creamy using Bamboo Spoon. Add egg and vanilla and beat well.

3 Add flour mixture to butter mixture and mix well. Stir in chocolate morsels.

4 Shape dough into a ball and place in center of **13" Round Baking Stone**. Lightly flour your hands and pat dough into an 11-inch circle. Place Baking Stone in **Oven-To-Table Rack**.

5 *Adult help:* Bake 14-16 minutes or until light golden brown. Using **Oven Mitts**, remove Baking Stone to **Nonstick Cooling Rack**. Cool completely.

6 Using **Skinny Scraper**, spread cooled cookie with frosting. To decorate, use **The Corer™** to cut round pieces from fruit rolls to resemble pepperoni. Using **Kitchen Shears**, snip gumdrops into pieces for pizza toppings. Add candy-coated chocolate pieces, as desired. Using **Deluxe Cheese Grater** fitted with fine grating drum, grate white chocolate over top for cheese. Cut into wedges with **Pizza Cutter**.

Approximately 310 calories and 16 grams of fat per serving

Cook's Tip:

BE CREATIVE WHEN DECORATING THIS GIANT COOKIE. USE YOUR FAVORITE FLAVOR OF FROSTING AND TRY DECORATING WITH OTHER CANDIES, SPRINKLES, COLORED SUGARS OR TINTED COCONUT.

Giant Pizza Cookie

Gingerbread Treasure Box p. 82, Chocolate-Dipped Spoons p. 83

Let's Celebrate!

From parties and picnics to holidays filled with traditions, fun-filled celebrations begin in the kitchen.

Gingerbread Treasure Box

GET THE WHOLE FAMILY TOGETHER TO MAKE THESE
EDIBLE CANDY- OR COOKIE-FILLED TREASURES.

MAKES 1 BOX

Ingredients:

½ RECIPE OF GINGERBREAD DOUGH
(SEE FAMILY HERITAGE™ HOME
TOWN INSTRUCTIONS
BROCHURE)

1 RECIPE OF ROYAL ICING (SEE
BROCHURE)

PEPPERMINT CANDY CANES (IF
DESIRED)

ASSORTED HOLIDAY CANDIES

Tools:

FAMILY HERITAGE™ HOME TOWN
GINGERBREAD HOUSE OR
SCHOOL/POST OFFICE MOLD

SERRATED BREAD KNIFE

OVEN MITTS

NONSTICK COOLING RACK

6" X 7" CARDBOARD COVERED
WITH FOIL

1 Preheat oven to 350°F. Lightly spray **Gingerbread House Mold** or **Gingerbread School/Post Office Mold** with non-stick cooking spray.

2 *Adult help:* Divide all ingredients for Gingerbread Recipe in half except use 1 egg; prepare dough according to recipe directions. Shape dough into a ball and divide into 2 portions. Wrap 1 portion in plastic wrap and refrigerate while working with the other portion.

3 To use **Gingerbread House Mold:** Press 1 portion of dough firmly into sections for roof, lower part of side wall (up to the bottom of the roof triangle) and front wall (this will be the box bottom). Do not fill chimney, snowman or tree sections. To use **Gingerbread School/Post Office Mold:** Press 1 portion of dough firmly into sections for roof, first story of the front wall and the side wall (this will be the box bottom). Do not fill flag, bell and banner sections. Holding **Serrated Bread Knife** parallel to surface of the mold, cut excess dough from mold.

4 *Adult help:* Bake 17-20 minutes or until edges are lightly browned. Using **Oven Mitts,** remove to **Nonstick Cooling Rack.** Cool in mold 5 minutes. Carefully remove cookie pieces from mold; cool completely.

5 Cool mold completely before filling with remaining dough. If using House Mold, use remaining dough to fill sections for roof and lower part of side wall (up to the bottom of the roof triangle). If using

School/Post Office Mold, use remaining dough to fill roof and first story of front wall. Trim excess dough. Bake and cool as directed in step 4.

6 *Adult help:* Prepare Royal Icing Recipe according to directions. Attach **Large Star Tip** to Decorating Bag according to directions and fill bag with icing.

7 To assemble: Place piece being used for box bottom on cardboard. Squeeze icing along the lower inside edge (the side with no pattern) of each piece being used for box sides and ends; press onto outside edges of box bottom. (There will be some space at each corner where pieces don't quite meet.) Prop with custard cups to hold pieces securely in place during drying. Fill space at each outside corner of box with icing. Place candy canes at corners, if desired. Let box stand until icing is completely dry (about ½ hour). Decorate outside of box with icing and assorted candies. Let dry.

Chocolate-Dipped Spoons

PICTURED ON PAGE 80

DIPPED IN SILKY-SMOOTH CHOCOLATE, OUR BAMBOO SPOONERS
MAKE A WONDERFUL GIFT FOR SOMEONE SPECIAL.

MAKES 6 CHOCOLATE-DIPPED SPOONS AND ABOUT 18 COOKIES

Ingredients:

- 1 CUP SEMI-SWEET CHOCOLATE MORSELS
- 1 TEASPOON VEGETABLE OIL
- SPRINKLE DECORATIONS, COLORED SPRINKLES OR NONPAREILS (IF DESIRED)
- 18 ASSORTED COOKIES SUCH AS BUTTER COOKIES, VANILLA WAFERS, COOKIE STICKS OR SHORTBREAD COOKIES

Tools:

ADJUSTABLE SCOOP
ADJUSTABLE MEASURING SPOON
COVERED MICRO-COOKER®
SKINNY SCRAPER
BAMBOO SPOONERS™ (6)

1 Place chocolate morsels and oil in **Covered Micro-Cooker®.** Do not cover. Microwave on HIGH 1 minute; stir with **Skinny Scraper.** Continue to microwave 10 seconds at a time, stirring after each 10 seconds, just until morsels are melted when stirred. Cover large tray with wax paper.

2 Holding handle of Micro-Cooker, tip container slightly toward you as you dip each **Bamboo Spooner™** into chocolate. Twist Spooner to evenly coat the bowl of the spoon. After dipping, gently tap handle of Spooner against edge of Micro-Cooker to remove the extra chocolate. Place Spooners on the wax paper. Sprinkle with decorations before chocolate sets. (If chocolate mixture becomes too thick for dipping, microwave on HIGH 10 seconds; stir and continue.)

3 One at a time, dip half of each cookie in remaining chocolate. Scrape bottom of cookie across top edge of Micro-Cooker to remove the extra chocolate. Place on wax paper and decorate, if desired. Refrigerate Spooners and cookies 30 minutes to allow chocolate to set up.

4 To give as gifts, wrap each Spooner separately in cellophane and tie with a ribbon. Package cookies as desired. Store Spooners and cookies in a cool dry place. Use Chocolate-Dipped Spoons to stir coffee or hot chocolate.

Cook's Tip:

MINT FLAVORED SEMI-SWEET CHOCOLATE MORSELS OR MILK CHOCOLATE MORSELS CAN ALSO BE USED.

I Scream, You Scream, Ice Cream Cake

I Scream, You Scream, Ice Cream Cake

CELEBRATE A BIRTHDAY OR ANY SPECIAL DAY WITH THIS SPECTACULAR, YET EASY, ICE CREAM, COOKIES AND CANDY "CAKE."

MAKES 12 SERVINGS

Ingredients:

- 15 CHOCOLATE CREAM-FILLED SANDWICH COOKIES
- 3 TABLESPOONS BUTTER OR MARGARINE
- 2 FAVORITE CANDY BARS (ABOUT 2 OUNCES EACH)
- 2 QUARTS OR 1 HALF-GALLON ANY FLAVOR(S) ICE CREAM
- 1 CONTAINER (12 OUNCES) FROZEN WHIPPED TOPPING, THAWED
- MULTICOLORED SPRINKLES OR SMALL CANDY DECORATIONS

Tools:

FOOD CHOPPER
13" X 9" CUTTING BOARD
COVERED MICRO-COOKER®
MY SAFE CUTTER™
BAMBOO SPOON
SPRINGFORM PAN SET
KITCHEN SHEARS
GARNISHER OR CRINKLE CUTTER
ALL-PURPOSE SPREADER
EASY ACCENT® DECORATOR
SLICE 'N SERVE®

1 On **Cutting Board,** finely chop cookies, 2-3 at a time, using **Food Chopper.** Place butter in **Covered Micro-Cooker®.** Microwave on HIGH 30 seconds or until melted. Mix in cookie crumbs with **Bamboo Spoon.** Press crumb mixture onto bottom of **Springform Pan.** Freeze 15 minutes.

2 Using **My Safe Cutter™,** cut each candy bar into 4 pieces; chop using Food Chopper.

3 Using **Kitchen Shears,** cut ice cream container(s) apart to expose block of ice cream. Using **Garnisher** or **Crinkle Cutter,** cut half of ice cream into 1-inch-thick slices. Arrange ice cream slices over cookie crust, cutting pieces to fit. Spread into a smooth layer with **All-Purpose Spreader.** Sprinkle with chopped candy bar. Top with remaining ice cream prepared the same way as first layer. Smooth top with spreader. Cover with aluminum foil. Freeze 3 hours or overnight.

4 Attach **Open Star Tip** to **Easy Accent®** Decorator. Fill tube with whipped topping and set aside. Run My Safe Cutter™ around edge of ice cream cake. Release collar from pan. Using spreader, frost top and side of ice cream cake with whipped topping. Decorate with whipped topping using decorator. Top with sprinkles. Freeze 1 hour or overnight. Once whipped topping is frozen, lightly cover cake with plastic wrap.

5 *Adult help:* To serve, cut into wedges using **Slice 'N Serve®.** (If cake was frozen overnight, place in refrigerator 10 minutes before slicing.)

Approximately 500 calories and 31 grams of fat per serving

Cook's Tip

TO MAKE THE CANDY BAR PIECES EASIER TO CHOP, WRAP THEM IN PLASTIC WRAP AND FREEZE FOR 10 MINUTES.

Valentine Sweet Heart

WITH A HEART AS BIG AS THIS, THERE'S PLENTY OF ROOM FOR FROSTING, DECORATING AND A SPECIAL MESSAGE.

MAKES 12 SERVINGS

Ingredients:

- 3 CUPS CRISPY RICE CEREAL
- 6 OUNCES (3 SQUARES) VANILLA ALMOND BARK
- ¼ CUP CREAMY PEANUT BUTTER
- ¾ CUP PREPARED VANILLA OR CHERRY FROSTING
- ASSORTED SMALL CANDIES

Tools:

ADJUSTABLE SCOOP
MEASURE-ALL® CUP
SUPER SCRAPER
SPRINGFORM PAN SET
KITCHEN SPRITZER
CLASSIC 2-QT. BATTER BOWL
COVERED MICRO-COOKER®
MIX 'N SCRAPER®
EASY ACCENT® DECORATOR
SERRATED BREAD KNIFE

1 Place **Heart-Shaped Insert** inside **Springform Pan.** Lightly spray inside of insert and bottom of pan with vegetable oil using **Kitchen Spritzer.**

2 Measure cereal into **Classic 2-Qt. Batter Bowl.**

3 Place almond bark and peanut butter in **Covered Micro-Cooker®.** Microwave, uncovered, on HIGH 1 minute. Stir with **Mix 'N Scraper®.** Continue microwaving 15-30 seconds or until mixture is melted and smooth when stirred.

4 Pour almond bark mixture over cereal and mix well. Pour mixture into heart insert. Press firmly with back of scraper. Refrigerate 30 minutes to set.

5 Remove the collar and insert from the springform pan; place heart on a serving plate. Attach **Round Tip** to **Easy Accent® Decorator.** Fill tube with frosting and write a special message. Change decorating tip as desired and make a border with frosting. Add candies as you like. Cut with **Serrated Bread Knife** to serve.

Approximately 200 calories and 9 grams of fat per serving

Cook's Tip:

ALMOND BARK IS A CANDY COATING THAT CAN BE FOUND IN THE BAKING SECTION OF YOUR SUPERMARKET. MAKE SURE ANY TOOLS USED FOR MELTING OR STIRRING ALMOND BARK ARE DRY OR THE MELTED MIXTURE CAN SEPARATE.

Tool Tip:

USE OUR HANDY **MEASURE-ALL® CUP** FOR MEASURING PEANUT BUTTER.

The Big Breakfast Omelet

JUMP START YOUR MORNING WITH THIS EASY
OVEN OMELET AND A SIDE OF FRESH FRUIT.

MAKES 8 SERVINGS

Ingredients:

- 2 TABLESPOONS BUTTER OR MARGARINE
- 2½ CUPS FROZEN SOUTHERN-STYLE HASH BROWN POTATOES
- 8 OUNCES DELI HAM, CUT ½ INCH THICK
- 3 GREEN ONIONS WITH TOPS
- 1 JAR (8 OUNCES) PROCESS CHEESE SAUCE
- 6 EGGS
- ⅓ CUP MILK

Tools:

- COVERED MICRO-COOKER®
- DEEP DISH BAKER
- 13" X 9" CUTTING BOARD
- GARNISHER OR CRINKLE CUTTER
- QUIKUT PARING KNIFE
- CLASSIC 2-QT. BATTER BOWL
- 10" WHISK
- OVEN MITTS
- STONEWARE TRIVET
- SLICE 'N SERVE®

1 Preheat oven to 350°F. Place butter in **Covered Micro-Cooker®**. Microwave on HIGH 1 minute or until melted; pour butter into **Deep Dish Baker**.

2 Place potatoes in bottom of Baker. On **Cutting Board,** cut ham into ½-inch cubes using **Garnisher** or **Crinkle Cutter** to get 1½ cups. Cut root end off green onions and thinly slice with **Quikut Paring Knife.** Sprinkle ham and onions evenly over potatoes.

3 Spoon process cheese sauce into **Classic 2-Qt. Batter Bowl.** Using **10" Whisk**, add eggs, 2 at a time, whisking until smooth. Gradually whisk in milk until well blended. Pour egg mixture over onions and ham.

4 *Adult help:* Bake 35 minutes or until set. Using **Oven Mitts**, remove to **Stoneware Trivet.** Let stand 5 minutes. Cut into wedges and serve using **Slice 'N Serve®.**

Approximately 190 calories and 13 grams of fat per serving

Savory Sausage Omelet:
Use 5 fully cooked maple-flavored sausage links, cut into slices instead of the ham.

Spring Bonnet Cake

Spring Bonnet Cake

SAY "HAPPY MOTHER'S DAY" WITH THIS DELIGHTFUL CAKE DECORATED WITH ALREADY PREPARED FROSTING AND PASTEL CANDIES.

MAKES 12-15 SERVINGS

Ingredients:

- 1 PACKAGE (18.25 OUNCES) YELLOW CAKE MIX (PLUS INGREDIENTS TO MAKE CAKE)
- 1 CONTAINER (16 OUNCES) PREPARED VANILLA FROSTING
- FOOD COLOR (IF DESIRED)
- 13 VANILLA CREAM-FILLED SANDWICH COOKIES
- 2 FRUIT SNACK ROLLS (3 FEET LONG EACH) IN DESIRED COLOR
- ASSORTED CANDIES
- CANDY SPEARMINT LEAVES

Tools:

- MEASURE-ALL® CUP
- CLASSIC 2-QT. BATTER BOWL
- CAKE TESTER
- OVEN MITTS
- NONSTICK COOLING RACK
- SKINNY SCRAPER
- EASY ACCENT® DECORATOR
- KITCHEN SHEARS

1 Preheat oven to 350°F. Spray inside of **Classic 2-Qt. Batter Bowl** with nonstick cooking spray.

2 Prepare cake mix according to package directions and pour into Batter Bowl.

3 *Adult help:* Bake 55-60 minutes or until **Cake Tester** inserted in center comes out clean. Using **Oven Mitts**, remove to **Nonstick Cooling Rack.** Cool cake in Batter Bowl 15 minutes. Turn over Batter Bowl onto Cooling Rack and remove Bowl. Cool completely before decorating.

4 To assemble bonnet, set cake with the large end down on a serving tray. Color frosting with food color, if desired. Using **Skinny Scraper,** spread cake with two thirds of the frosting. Surround cake with cookies to form a brim for bonnet.

5 To decorate bonnet, remove fruit roll from paper. Starting at center of fruit roll, place fruit roll around bottom of cake, crisscrossing ends, to resemble a ribbon. Make a bow with remaining fruit roll and place at crisscross. Trim ends of "ribbons" with **Kitchen Shears.** Use candies to make flowers on bonnet. Cut spearmint leaves in half with Kitchen Shears and add to flowers.

6 To decorate brim, attach **Open Star Tip** to **Easy Accent® Decorator** and fill tube with remaining frosting. Decorate brim of bonnet.

Approximately 440 calories and 18 grams of fat per serving

Dad's Fishing Hat:

Assemble cake with cookie brim as directed and frost cake. Decorate with candy gummy fish and worms. Use just 1 fruit roll to make a hat-band, trimming the ends. Use your imagination!

Firecracker Ice

YOUR TASTE BUDS WILL EXPLODE WITH REALLY COOL
FRUITY FLAVOR WHEN YOU EAT THIS ICY TREAT.

MAKES 8 SERVINGS

Ingredients:

1 ENVELOPE (.18 OUNCE)
   STRAWBERRY FLAVOR (OR ANY
   RED COLOR) UNSWEETENED
   POWDERED SOFT DRINK MIX

1 ENVELOPE (.18 OUNCE) BERRY
   FLAVOR (OR ANY BLUE COLOR)
   UNSWEETENED POWDERED
   SOFT DRINK MIX

1 ENVELOPE (.26 OUNCE) LEMONADE
   FLAVOR UNSWEETENED
   POWDERED SOFT DRINK MIX

   WATER

1 CAN (14 OUNCES) SWEETENED
   CONDENSED MILK

   SUGAR CONES (IF DESIRED)

Tools:

ICE SHAVER WITH TUBS
ADJUSTABLE MEASURING SPOONS
CAN OPENER
CLASSIC 2-QT. BATTER BOWL
MEASURE-ALL® CUP
10" WHISK
MEDIUM STAINLESS STEEL SCOOP
CHILLZANNE® MINI-BOWL

1 Measure out 1 teaspoon strawberry flavor drink mix and place in 1 **Ice Shaver Tub.** Add 1 tablespoon water and stir until completely dissolved. In second tub, dissolve 1 teaspoon berry flavor drink mix in 1 tablespoon water. Repeat procedure using 1 teaspoon lemonade flavor drink mix and 1 tablespoon water in third tub.

2 In **Classic 2-Qt. Batter Bowl,** whisk sweetened condensed milk and 2½ cups water using **10" Whisk** until well blended. Pour 1¼ cups of the milk mixture into each tub, stirring gently until liquid is all one color. Cover tubs with lids and place in freezer. Freeze until firm (about 6 hours).

3 *Adult help:* Place **Chillzanne® Mini-Bowl** under **Ice Shaver** to catch shavings. Remove frozen mixture from 1 tub and shave with Ice Shaver. (Never put fingers into Ice Shaver!) Repeat with remaining tubs.

4 Using medium **Stainless Steel Scoop,** scoop shaved ices into serving dishes or sugar cones, if desired.

Approximately 160 calories and 4 grams of fat per serving

Cook's Tips:

USE LEFTOVER DRINK MIX TO MAKE AN 8-OUNCE GLASS OF FRUIT DRINK. FOR EACH FLAVOR, MIX THE REMAINING DRINK MIX WITH 1 CUP OF COLD WATER AND 3 TABLESPOONS OF SUGAR. ADD AN EXTRA TABLESPOON OF SUGAR FOR THE LEMONADE FLAVOR.

TO EASILY REMOVE FROZEN MIXTURES FROM ICE SHAVER TUBS, HOLD TUBS UNDER COOL RUNNING WATER FOR A FEW SECONDS.

Tool Tip:

THE CHILLZANNE® MINI-BOWL IS AN IDEAL CONTAINER TO USE WHEN SHAVING ICES. POP IT INTO THE FREEZER AT THE SAME TIME AS THE ICE SHAVER TUBS AND IT WILL BE READY TO GO. STORE LEFTOVER FIRECRACKER ICE IN COVERED BOWL IN THE FREEZER.

Firecracker Ice

Cookie Pops

BAKE UP SOME FUN WITH THESE EASY-TO-MAKE-
AND-DECORATE COOKIES ON A STICK!

MAKES 16 COOKIES

Ingredients:

1 PACKAGE (18 OUNCES)
  REFRIGERATED SUGAR
  COOKIE DOUGH

16 FLAT WOODEN STICKS

GRANULATED SUGAR

PREPARED VANILLA OR
  CHOCOLATE FROSTING

LARGE MARSHMALLOWS,
  COLORED SUGARS, SPRINKLES,
  NONPAREILS OR CANDIES FOR
  DECORATING

Tools:

13" X 9" CUTTING BOARD

KITCHEN SHEARS

QUIKUT PARING KNIFE

15" ROUND BAKING STONE
  WITH OVEN-TO-TABLE RACK

MEASURE-ALL® CUP

OVEN MITTS

OVEN PAD

NONSTICK COOLING RACK

MINI-SERVING SPATULA

EASY ACCENT® DECORATOR

1 Preheat oven to 350°F. Place packaged refrigerated cookie dough on **Cutting Board.** Using **Kitchen Shears**, cut off package ends and cut open along seam. Cut dough into sixteen ½-inch-thick slices using **Quikut Paring Knife.** Use your hands to shape each slice of dough into a ball.

2 Place 8 balls of cookie dough 3 inches apart and 2 inches from edge on **15" Round Baking Stone.** Insert sticks sideways into balls, pointing ends toward center of Baking Stone. Flatten balls slightly using bottom of **Measure-All® Cup** dipped in granulated sugar. Place Baking Stone in **Oven-To-Table Rack.**

3 *Adult help:* Bake 14-16 minutes or until light golden brown. Using **Oven Mitts**, remove to **Oven Pad.** Cool cookies on Baking Stone 2-3 minutes. Use **Mini-Serving Spatula** to transfer cookies to **Nonstick Cooling Rack.** Cool completely.

4 Repeat steps #2 and #3 for remaining cookie dough.

5 Attach desired tip to **Easy Accent® Decorator** and fill tube with frosting. Decorate cookies with frosting and candies as desired. Use your imagination to create flowers, smiley faces, baseballs, soccer balls and more!

Approximately 130 calories and 5 grams of fat per serving (1 undecorated cookie)

Cook's Tips:

TO MAKE COOKIES WITH MARSH-MALLOW FLOWERS, SNIP EACH MARSHMALLOW CROSSWISE INTO 4 SLICES USING **KITCHEN SHEARS.** DIP A STICKY SIDE INTO COLORED SUGAR OR NONPAREILS, IF DESIRED. SQUEEZE FROSTING ONTO COOKIES THEN ADD 5-6 MARSHMALLOW SLICES TO EACH COOKIE TO CREATE FLOWER PETALS; FILL CENTERS WITH FROSTING OR CANDY PIECES. TIE GREEN RIBBONS AROUND STICKS TO RESEMBLE LEAVES, IF DESIRED.

TO PREPARE COLORED FROSTING, ADD A FEW DROPS OF FOOD COLORING TO VANILLA FROSTING TO GET DESIRED COLOR.

Cheery Cherry Apple Crisp

THIS DESSERT SAYS IT ALL—
"HOME SWEET HOME."

MAKES 8 SERVINGS

Ingredients:

FRUIT FILLING

1 CAN (30 OUNCES) CHERRY PIE
FILLING

3 LARGE GRANNY SMITH APPLES
(1½ POUNDS)

TOPPING

¾ CUP ALL-PURPOSE FLOUR

½ CUP QUICK OR OLD-FASHIONED
OATS

⅓ CUP PACKED BROWN SUGAR

½ TEASPOON GROUND CINNAMON

DASH OF SALT

⅓ CUP STICK BUTTER OR
MARGARINE

VANILLA ICE CREAM OR THAWED
FROZEN WHIPPED TOPPING
(IF DESIRED)

Tools:

CAN OPENER

ADJUSTABLE SCOOP

ADJUSTABLE MEASURING SPOON

QUIKUT PARING KNIFE

13" X 9" CUTTING BOARD

BAMBOO SPOON

9" SQUARE BAKER

APPLE PEELER/CORER/SLICER

1-QT. BATTER BOWL

COVERED MICRO-COOKER®

OVEN MITTS

OVEN PAD

ICE CREAM DIPPER

1 Preheat oven to 375°F. For fruit filling, spoon pie filling into **9" Square Baker** using **Bamboo Spoon** and set aside.

2 *Adult help:* Peel, core and slice apples using **Apple Peeler/Corer/Slicer** and place apples on **Cutting Board**. Cut apples in quarters using **Quikut Paring Knife.**

3 Mix apples into pie filling and set aside.

4 For topping, mix flour, oats, brown sugar, cinnamon and salt in **1-Qt. Batter Bowl** using Bamboo Spoon.

5 Place butter in **Covered Micro-Cooker®**. Microwave on HIGH 1 minute or until melted. Stir butter into flour mixture in Batter Bowl and mix well. Sprinkle topping evenly over fruit filling in Baker.

6 *Adult help:* Bake 40 minutes or until topping is deep golden brown. Using **Oven Mitts**, remove Baker to **Oven Pad**. Serve warm with a scoop of ice cream or dollop of whipped topping, if desired.

Approximately 310 calories and 9 grams of fat per serving

Itsy, Bitsy Spiders

Itsy, Bitsy Spiders

CREATE THESE TINY CRITTERS
COMPLETE WITH THEIR OWN WEB!

MAKES 12 SERVINGS (24 SPIDERS AND ONE 8-INCH SPIDER WEB)

Ingredients:

- 1 BOX (14 OUNCES) PUMPKIN QUICK BREAD MIX (PLUS INGREDIENTS TO MAKE BREAD)
- 1 CUP PREPARED VANILLA FROSTING
- YELLOW AND RED LIQUID FOOD COLOR
- RED, BLACK OR PURPLE STRING OR PULL APART LICORICE
- 48 CHOCOLATE COVERED RAISINS, SMALL BLACK JELLY BEANS OR SEMI-SWEET CHOCOLATE MORSELS

Tools:

MEASURE-ALL® CUP
DELUXE MINI-MUFFIN PAN
8" MINI-BAKER
CLASSIC 2-QT. BATTER BOWL
BAMBOO SPOON
SMALL STAINLESS STEEL SCOOP
SUPER SCRAPER
CAKE TESTER
OVEN MITTS
NONSTICK COOLING RACK
EASY ACCENT® DECORATOR
KITCHEN SHEARS

1 Preheat oven to 325°F. Spray cups of **Deluxe Mini-Muffin Pan** and **8" Mini-Baker** with nonstick cooking spray.

2 In **Classic 2-Qt. Batter Bowl**, prepare mix according to package directions for bread using **Bamboo Spoon**.

3 Using small **Stainless Steel Scoop**, fill each Mini-Muffin cup with 1 scoop of batter. Spread remaining batter into Mini-Baker using **Super Scraper**.

4 *Adult help:* Bake muffins 13-15 minutes and bread 25-30 minutes or until **Cake Tester** inserted in centers comes out clean. Using **Oven Mitts**, remove to **Nonstick Cooling Rack**. Cool muffins and bread 15 minutes each. Remove from pan and Baker. Cool completely.

5 Attach **Round Tip** to **Easy Accent® Decorator** and fill tube with ⅓ cup frosting. Place bread on serving tray. Squeeze out frosting to make a spider web design.

6 Squeeze out frosting left in decorator and add to remaining ⅔ cup of frosting. Use food colors to color frosting orange (see Cook's Tip). Attach **Open Star Tip** to decorator and fill tube with frosting. Swirl frosting over tops of muffins. Using **Kitchen Shears**, cut licorice into 2-inch pieces. For each spider, press 8 licorice pieces into frosting for legs; add 2 raisins for eyes. Arrange spiders on serving tray around web.

Approximately 300 calories and 9 grams of fat per serving

Cook's Tip:

TO MAKE FROSTING ORANGE, USE ABOUT TWICE AS MANY DROPS OF YELLOW COLOR AS RED AND STIR THOROUGHLY. PASTE FOOD COLORS CAN ALSO BE USED. COOKING TRULY IS AN ART!

Index